D0871879

Books by John E. Mack
Nightmares and Human Conflict
Borderline States in Psychiatry
  (Edited by Dr. Mack)
A Prince of Our Disorder: The Life of T. E. Lawrence

Books by Holly Hickler
Creative Writing: From Thought to Action
  (With C. Lowell May)
Expository Writing: From Thought to Action
  (With C. Lowell May)

Vivienne

Vivienne

JOHN E. MACK
HOLLY HICKLER

The Life and Suicide of an Adolescent Girl

Little, Brown and Company   Boston / Toronto

PROPERTY OF

Copyright © 1981 by John E. Mack and Holly Hickler
Poetry, letters, school compositions, and journal entries by
Vivienne Loomis copyright © 1981 by David Loomis and
Paulette Loomis

All rights reserved. No part of this book may be reproduced
in any form or by any electronic or mechanical means including information storage and retrieval systems without
permission in writing from the publisher, except by a re-
viewer who may quote brief passages in a review.

First Edition

LIBRARY OF CONGRESS CATALOGING IN PUBLICATION DATA

Mack, John E., 1929–
    Vivienne: the life and suicide of an adolescent girl.

    Bibliography: p.
    1. Loomis, Vivienne, 1959–1973.   2. Adolescent
girls — United States — Biography.   3. Youth — United
States — Suicidal behavior.   I. Hickler, Holly.
II. Title.
HV6546.L66M3   616.85′844509   [B]   81-11752
ISBN 0-316-54228-8   AACR2

Quotations from the letters, journal entries, and school compositions appearing in this book are reprinted by permission
of the copyright holders.

MV

Designed by Susan Windheim

Published simultaneously in Canada
by Little, Brown & Company (Canada) Limited

PRINTED IN THE UNITED STATES OF AMERICA

Contents

What is it?
The stillness of wisdom?
The patience of doom?
That drives you to mount
That coal-black stallion?

Why is it
That you suddenly know
With certainty
That you cannot stay astride?

from "Dream of Reality"
Vivienne Loomis
July 10, 1973

Introduction

INCREASING NUMBERS of American youth choose to end their lives through suicide. For the clinician, as Alfred Alvarez wrote in *The Savage God*, "The successful suicide is, in every sense, beyond him." [1] Many practitioners have regretted that there seems no way to study completed suicides. Reports about patients who have killed themselves are rare. The loss of a patient through suicide, especially a very young person, is such a painful experience for a psychotherapist that few have written about what they learned.

Nor do today's teachers, who "are often among the very first individuals who have an opportunity to recognize the symptoms of depression" and other indicators of possible suicide, catch important signals in troubled adolescents. Schools don't offer the suicidal teenager "the possibility of establishing and perpetuating meaningful relationships." [2]

There are psychotic adolescents who kill themselves, others who seem to act impulsively, or lose their lives in accidents in which self-destructive forces are operating. But the great majority premeditate their act, as Vivienne Loomis did, over a substantial period of time. Albert Camus observed, "An act like this is prepared within the silence of the heart, as is a great work of art." ³

Memoirs, autobiographies and diaries have often provided rich psychological insight, particularly when they offer thoughts and feelings not otherwise shared. Early adolescence is a time of great reticence in which young people may have intense difficulty revealing their inner lives, especially to an adult. This is one reason teenagers often begin to communicate their private thoughts and feelings to a diary.

Vivienne was fourteen years and four months old when she hanged herself. She left behind a diary — she called it "My Private Paper Book" — that no one read before her death. It provides a chronicle of her inner experience during the three years before she killed herself, after several aborted attempts. Vivienne left many poems, school compositions, and a number of letters to one of her teachers, which help us understand her inner life during these three years. These writings, together with tape-recorded interviews with Vivienne's parents, her brother and sister, the schoolteacher, and the friend to whom she confided her suicidal preoccupations during the last three months of her life, constitute the principal data for this book.

In his pioneering paper on depression, "Mourning and Melancholia," Freud said of suicide, "We have never been able to explain what interplay of forces can carry such a purpose through to execution." ⁴ In this book we are concerned with the "interplay of forces" in Vivienne's life, especially between the inner emotional life and social reality. Vivienne, who died in 1973, was very much a child of her era, unusually sensitive to the world around her. The nature of that world, as well as the sensitivity with which she responded to its pressures, bears on the problem of her suicide.

When we began to study Vivienne's written legacy, both of us were impressed with the intricacy of her personality and the depth of her emotional experience. It was unexpected in one so young. In this regard, Vivienne may have been atypical. Also, we wondered if we could expect to reach conclusions about adolescent suicide from the case of one young girl, no matter how detailed. We do suspect, however, that the elements of Vivienne's history and experience are common enough to justify our hope that this work may contribute insights useful to others and generate hypotheses and further research into the problem of suicide, particularly adolescent suicide.

The collection of Vivienne's work started the summer after she died. Holly Hickler, a teacher at Cambridge School of Weston, called Vivienne's mother, Paulette Loomis, and expressed her interest in Vivienne's writing. Paulette had been thinking of producing a handcrafted volume for the family, but as the project was discussed, both women became excited about arranging for publication. New material was discovered, and together they began to assemble the work chronologically. For two years, the work went on until Holly Hickler had a final manuscript. It was to be an anthology of Vivienne's writing. Paulette and Holly were considering this format when John Mack unexpectedly entered the picture.

Planning a lecture on normal adolescent behavior, Mack asked one of his sons, then a sophomore at Cambridge School, if he knew a creative-writing teacher likely to have assigned papers to her students that would encourage them to write candidly about themselves. He suggested Holly Hickler, who had collected boxes of student writing to be used in a series of textbooks she was publishing with another teacher. She made these available to John Mack and then showed him her special carton of Vivienne's work. He was instantly struck by the quality and uniqueness of the collection and proposed a design for the book that led to its publication.

Ironically, among Holly's rich file of essays, the ones that seemed most vividly and clearly to illustrate the everyday struggles of adolescents to get along with parents, friends and teachers, and to clarify their feelings about identity, self-worth, sexual morality and other personal values, even about the use of drugs, were Vivienne's. John Mack based his lecture largely on these writings of hers, omitting the most patently troubled ones. No one in the audience, which included many professional clinicians experienced in work with adolescents, suspected that the writings were those of a depressed child, much less one who had committed suicide. This suggested several questions: Does depression grow out of the intensified experience of common developmental issues that the adolescent lacks personal resources to handle? Or is a child who sees so clearly and feels so deeply more likely to be overwhelmed by the painful dilemmas with which most adolescents wrestle more successfully? Is it possible that the pain of a troubled adolescent's struggles encourages the development of an introspective trend? All of these possibilities might be true.

Vivienne was not an odd or strange child. There is much in this book that attests to her humor, her wisdom and empathy. Even her depression and suicide can be understood in relation to the developmental struggles all adolescents face. It was this fact that led us, finally, to tell her story, to break for her "the silence of the heart."

An important collaboration in the development of this work has been with Vivienne's family: her parents, David and Paulette Loomis, her brother, Rob, and her sister, Laurel. This book is dedicated to them.

It is to their credit that the Loomises agreed to let us publish Vivienne's story. Many families who have lost a treasured member through suicide do not wish to think about the experience or talk about it with others. The Loomises' courage has been inspiring.

Vivienne's death left her parents with an overwhelming sense of loss and guilt. David found, nearly four years later, that only the language of ancient religion could describe his emotions.

He knew what it was, he said, to feel "just utterly damned." Nothing can assuage such anguish, can erase such feelings. But it is the Loomises' hope — and ours — that we may shed some light on Vivienne's life and death, give them meaning, and relieve at least the pointlessness of this loss.

This three-sided collaboration among a teacher, a family and a clinician has given the book its shape and direction. It is written with the hope that it can be meaningful to anyone close to adolescents: therapists and counselors, teachers whose daily experience must include depressed young people, families struggling with the problem of adolescent suicide. We hope, too, that Vivienne can live again in these pages as the sensitive, remarkable young girl she was.

As writers, we have necessarily been selective in our portrayal of the Loomis family. In considering their tragedy we concentrated on the difficult struggles relating to Vivienne's depression and death. But this perspective, with its emphasis on conflict, in no way detracts from our belief that the Loomises are a family characterized by warmth, intelligence and deep moral concern. It is a tribute to them as a family and as individuals that they not only are willing to share their terrible loss but have continued to develop their own potentials. Each has found a useful and valuable place in our society.

The book is divided into two parts. The first contains the narrative of Vivienne's life and death, told as much as possible through her own words from her journal, poems, letters and school compositions. The second part is interpretive, an effort to understand the forces that led Vivienne to her decision and to consider her death in relation to the increasing national problem of adolescent suicide.

ONE

Vivienne

At 6:30 on the evening of December 21, 1973, Vivienne Loomis, an attractive ninth-grader, especially gifted in writing, hanged herself in her mother's empty silversmithing studio. She was fourteen years and four months old.

AT THE TIME of Vivienne's death her parents, David and Paulette Loomis — scheduled to move in a few days from their Melrose, Massachusetts, home to the seaport of Gloucester — were arriving at a farewell party in their honor, hardly a block away. Her older sister, Laurel, was playing the piano in the stripped-down living room at home. Her brother, Rob, was in his apartment in Revere and her best friend, Anne, was about to leave on a Christmas vacation trip with her parents. John May, an admired and important teacher, was three thousand miles away.

David Loomis had decided to leave his ministry in Melrose to take up the position offered him in a Unitarian-Universalist church in Gloucester, less than an hour's drive away. This had been a difficult decision, two years in the making. He was later to worry about its effect on Vivienne.

"Our home had been in turmoil preparing for our move to the new church and community. Packed cartons, pictures off the walls and shrouded in sheets, rugs rolled up ready to go, created a depressing sight," Paulette wrote in a memorial narrative.

"Everything was in boxes," Laurel said later. "Vivienne and I had had a terrific fight about packing. That week she refused to help. I just wanted to shut everything out. I often did that when I was upset. I would play the piano and get lost in the music. That's what I was doing that night. Mummy and Daddy had gone to the party. I was dimly aware of Vivienne. I saw her a couple of times. She walked downstairs, went upstairs, came down again and back up. I just didn't think about it. Finally she walked down to the basement. She must have been down there fifteen minutes when suddenly I thought, 'This is strange, something funny's going on here.' I had a kind of intuition it had happened. And I walked down and found her."

Laurel ran upstairs to the kitchen and grabbed a knife from one of the packed cartons. "I was yelling and screaming," Laurel said. "It sounds strange, I guess, but I was furious she had done it." She ran back to the basement and cut Vivienne down. Laurel tried to revive her sister but Vivienne was already dead.

"Fifteen minutes after we got there we got this frantic call," Paulette remembered. "It was Laurel. She was saying, 'Mom. Mom. Mom. Vivienne hung herself. Mom, I've been trying to —' I called the doctor and then I just ran. The doctor called the police, but the police car stopped at the wrong house. The rescue team stopped at the wrong house too, but it was all over. She was already gone."

On the day of Vivienne's death Paulette had been uneasy about her. "I was working six days that week to get time off for packing. I came home on my lunch hour that day, but Vivienne was still in bed. When I got home at suppertime she was sitting in the kitchen — just sitting there. I picked up her hair and gave her a big kiss on the back of the neck. She didn't respond at all. There was a funny smell about her. Now I realize it was the smell of fear. She had decided to do this thing and she had figured out the timing, but she was afraid."

Vivienne must have been planning her death several days

before. "I had given her the rope on Sunday," Paulette continued. "She asked me for some rope that day and I didn't even ask
why. I thought it had something to do with packing. I remembered that we had some L. L. Bean rope around somewhere
and I found it and that is what she used. I think she was down
there trying it that Sunday because I came down with a load of
wash for the washing machine and she was down there. I said,
'Are you getting some clothes or something?' She didn't say
much, she just went upstairs. There was only one room that
was totally cleaned out in preparation for the move. It was my
silversmithing shop. She used a water pipe in my shop and the
instrument I had put in her hands."

Why had Vivienne decided to die?

In the days that followed, everyone who had been close to
Vivienne suffered over this question. Laurel thought she had
been intolerably lonely. Paulette wondered if her child had had
a chemical imbalance. David worried that the family upsets
and the confusion of moving had been too much for her. Rob
wished he had been closer to the family. John May wondered
what he could have done. Anne felt that Vivienne was determined. "She thought of death as beautiful — like a cloud," Anne
said later.

Vivienne was the third child of thoughtful, intelligent parents.
Her father, a Unitarian minister, is a gentle, introspective man
with abundant gray hair, and warm blue eyes behind his glasses.
He serves as chaplain to the Falmouth Hospital in Falmouth,
Massachusetts, and offers one day a week to the nearby Barn-
stable Hospital. David Loomis is conscientiously fair-minded
and prone to seeing many sides of a question — so much so
that decisions are painfully difficult for him. Although this has,
at times, subjected the family to strain and uncertainty, both
Laurel and Rob often refer to their father's integrity. Vivienne's
mother is a craftsman and artist, a working metalsmith with a

strong drive for achievement and a taste for adventure. The daughter of a minister herself, Paulette is a tall, upright woman whose face is seldom in repose. Even in casual conversation, she looks directly into the eyes of her listener and leans characteristically slightly forward as she speaks. Her sentences are definite and crisp in contrast to her husband's soft-spoken, murmuring tone. Paulette's eyes are a dark, intense blue. She has worked off and on as a librarian, but dreams of leaving a beautiful work of art to posterity. "I wanted to leave something behind me that was unique," she declared. "And when I made silver I wanted to make something that would still be here in two thousand years, maybe in a museum someplace, but hopefully in my family."

Rob, the oldest of the children, now married, is a serious young man. He speaks thoughtfully and carefully with an eye to exactness and truth. He often gazes into the middle distance as he talks, as though something just beyond him is both puzzling and instructive. His love for music has led him to the art of harpsichord and piano restoration. Laurel is the middle child, eighteen months older than Vivienne. She looks at life with a forthrightness and courage that is tempered by special sensitivity. She has the delicate, fresh look of a Beardsley drawing. She is animated in conversation, frowning sometimes as she searches for her thought and then bursting forth again with new energy. The clarity of her coloring reminds one of porcelain in tinted pinks and cream. Her eyes are a startlingly light blue. Laurel has spent a year and a half in Holland learning frame weaving. She expects to continue her study in art school here.

From the time of her birth Vivienne was special, according to her mother. Even the delivery was unusual. "I was determined," Paulette said, "to use natural childbirth and I decided to be part of an experiment using music. All the time I was in labor I had on earphones. Vivienne's arrival was watched by as many hospital personnel as could crowd into the delivery room in their interest in the effects of music heard through earphones in lieu of anesthesia. Vivienne arrived, a chubby, purple baby whose tiny apricot tongue revealed the jaundice she had contracted when our incompatible blood types mixed." Vivienne was born to music on August 14, 1959.

From the beginning Paulette felt some alienation from this infant. At the same time Vivienne was, she said, "better than anything that ever came along in the family." She was a peaceable baby, unlike her older brother and sister. She looked, from the beginning, strikingly like baby pictures of her father. "We have some pictures of David that even Vivienne thought were pictures of her," Paulette said. As an infant Vivienne made very few demands and required less of her mother's attention than the others had. She was a quiet baby, "willing to be relegated to the playpen," her mother said. "You could give her a bunch of toys, a bottle of milk or some orange juice and she seemed perfectly happy." On the other hand, Rob and Laurel remember early childhood tantrums. "She would sit on the floor screaming for hours," Laurel said.

In the summer of 1961, when Vivienne was two, Paulette and David went to Europe for ten weeks. They took Rob with them but left Laurel and Vivienne with a baby-sitter who had stayed with the children in the past. When her parents returned, Vivienne seemed not to recognize her mother and for several days would have nothing to do with her.

"She could be stubborn," her mother said. When she was three, "I made them all matching Easter outfits for a fashion show. Vivienne didn't want to be in it. She just wasn't going to wear that dress. I have a picture of them all that shows Vivienne sticking out that stubborn lower lip." By this time Paulette felt that in a curious way Vivienne "already had tuned us out."

Vivienne showed early signs of unusual sensitivity. As a small child she had a rare ability to identify with the pain of others.

When she was four and a half, her mother's father was fatally stricken with a ruptured aortic aneurism. "We got into the car and took Vivienne with us," Paulette remembered. "It was a long ride to the hospital and halfway there I just knew my father had died. I got upset and Vivienne began to cry. She had a small gift she had made him. When we finally arrived at the hospital he was dead." Vivienne couldn't be comforted. A month later, a family friend visited the Loomises. Paulette spoke of how much she missed her father. "Vivienne cried and cried and cried," Paulette said. "It was just an outpouring. I remember sitting in the rocking chair and rocking her and rocking her. I thought she was going to be physically sick from the amount of crying she did." The memory of this grandfather was a powerful one for Vivienne. In a school essay, written two months before her death, she recalled him vividly:

> ... My grandfather comes back to me now, with his intensely gentle eyes and a strangely distorted face. An unconquered mind; I remember he always used to tell me that ... *dreams* were for pursuing. He is with me now, and he paints me his pictures of flat-tailed doves that glide purposefully over black and scrawny ravens who fight over death. And he shows me carefully, the valley where the two mountains of reason and emotion meet and twine their efforts together in winding streams that quietly defy your logic. But just as I relinquish my power to fight this strange current, and I feel the waters rush through my veins, my grandfather is leaving me ...

Seven months later, Vivienne's other grandfather died. Once again she seemed to absorb the family pain.

In the early years of Vivienne's life, the family lived in Winchendon in northern Massachusetts, a small mill town, mostly

Roman Catholic with a large French Canadian population. It was a town that was becoming increasingly impoverished. The year after Vivienne's birth, the mills moved south and the town became even more depressed. It was there that Vivienne and Laurel first attended public school. Rob, however, was sent to his maternal grandparents in Deerfield, Massachusetts, to attend a private elementary school, and came home on weekends. This arrangement lasted for three years, Rob's first, second, and third grades.

"I had to get him out of the house," Paulette explained. "He had problems with his father, acted out against the girls, and did nasty things behind my back."

Rob remembers this as a happy time. "My grandfather had always wanted a son — there he was. They really enjoyed me and I enjoyed them.... My grandfather ... was also a cabinet-maker and so I was interested in working with my hands.... I had someone waiting on me, wanting to know what I wanted to do." He was unaware until recently of the reason for his boarding situation. "I thought it was planned so I could go to a better school," he said.

Vivienne's first-grade experience in Winchendon seemed to set the scene for the misery she experienced in much of her subsequent time in public school. A year later the family moved to Melrose, a predominantly Catholic community to the north of Boston, where David began a new ministry.

"We were different from everyone else," Laurel recalls. "We wore old-fashioned dresses that Mummy smocked herself. Other girls wore smart shifts and the 'big thing' was to be dressed in earrings and stockings."

Vivienne had sucked her thumb until she had "rearranged her jaw," according to her mother, and by the second grade required the attention of an orthodontist, who fitted her with braces. Rob and Laurel remember the constant pain as the bands were tightened and how Vivienne dreaded her appointments. "It was four or five years of pain and humiliation," Laurel said. Vivienne also became increasingly bookish and did very well academically, which further set her apart as "different." "She always seemed to be the butt of playground jokes," Laurel remembers. Paulette said, "There was actually one neighborhood child who would walk a different way to school so as not to be seen with Vivienne. I think she was afraid of being ostracized as Vivienne was."

Laurel was more outgoing and made a few friends. "Vivienne just let Laurel do all the socializing for her. I think Vivienne felt awfully isolated and alone, but she didn't let you know any of that. She developed this sarcastic wit that could be devastating. I think it alienated other children even more. She gave back better than she got," Paulette commented. This verbal combativeness was a response to the family code against aggressive behavior, Rob felt. "We were never allowed to be physically violent or to swear," he said. "Verbalization and mediation were encouraged."

At home Vivienne showed a happier side of her nature when she was small, Paulette felt. She could be charming and humorous. Her mother considered her a "good girl" most of the time. By contrast Laurel and Rob were more unruly. "They were into everything," according to their mother. They occasionally took money from Paulette's wallet, for example. "Mummy spanked us a lot until she couldn't do it anymore." Laurel said, "We got old enough to hit back."

Paulette's life was a demanding one and she tackled it with characteristic energy. She was the mother of two lively, somewhat rebellious older children and an unusually sensitive youngest. She worked off and on as a librarian and attended to her many duties as a minister's wife. Money had to be handled carefully and inventively. Impatient by nature, she suffered through her husband's slow and extended decision-making. Nevertheless, she spent as much time as she could on her art. A graduate of Rhode Island School of Design, Paulette cherished ambitions to make jewelry, paint, sketch, and continue handicrafts. "I think Mummy resented having to spend years of energy on children instead of art," Rob reflected. Laurel felt that her mother was often abstracted, absorbed in her own struggles. "My mother was always sick, always tired . . . she needed attention," Laurel said. "Sometimes she got attention by making people feel guilty. She would make it seem that we were doing things to hurt her."

At the same time, both Rob and Laurel felt that their mother was keenly interested in their lives. "She wanted us to share everything and we did," Laurel said. There were times when both children felt little space or privacy was allowed them. As a result, when Rob and Laurel got older, they went out as much as they could. Vivienne stayed at home more. She read constantly as a child and she was on hand as a kind of adviser for her mother. "I thought of her as a confidante," Paulette said. "She was such a good listener and I was so worried about Rob and Laurel. I'd say to her, 'Well, what would you do —' and she'd give me advice." Later, Paulette was to reproach herself with the burden she may have placed on Vivienne.

While Paulette thought that the family life began to center on Laurel and Rob, Laurel had the impression that the household often revolved around Paulette's frame of mind. Both Rob and Laurel remember their mother as the source of power in their home. "Sometimes she would give Dad a direction to give us," Rob commented, and Laurel added, "Because she wanted Daddy to have some contact with us, some leadership"; but by and large both children think of their father as a listener, disinclined to take action. From almost the beginning, Vivienne seemed to feel an instinctive sympathy with her father. Her first journal entry, written at age nine on the way to Europe with her family, reveals her affection: "This KLM is huge! I've got a very comfortable place next to my lovely Dad! Mummy isn't feeling well. I'm sorry. I'm HAVING LOADS OF FUN THOUGH."

The differences between the two parents were impressive to Rob and Laurel, even as children. Paulette saw the contrast reflected in Vivienne's own nature. "She was just a combination of both of us," Paulette said. "She had half David's holding back and half of my pushing ahead. The conflict came to a head-on clash inside this kid and she didn't know how to deal with it. Part of me and part of her father in one skin! It could never be resolved."

Sharing, honesty, and the importance of being an individual were all family ideals. "There was a family tradition of being unique, even eccentric," Rob said. An uncle Justin on the mother's side is said to have been expelled from Lawrenceville Academy for leading a cow into the chapel belfry and tying its tail to the bell rope. The family Unitarianism stressed independence of mind and a questioning spirit. Individual soul-searching and an avoidance of ready answers were family characteristics. "We were always told," Laurel remembers, "that we should be proud of being ourselves, that we shouldn't copy others, and that we should be active in the community. Mummy used to say, 'You can do something, you can make a difference.' " This was put into action in the conservative suburb of Melrose. The family voted Democratic and their religion was Unitarian. "They were both about as popular as Communism in that neighborhood," Rob remarked. Nonetheless, the children were encouraged to political action early. In 1968 they worked in their neighborhood handing out leaflets for Eugene McCarthy.

Education was another strong family ideal. Although the family budget made it difficult, David and Paulette often considered private schools for the three children. "That's one gift we can give you, a gift we want to give you," Paulette told them.

In the fall of 1969 Rob was sent to Loomis School, an exclusive prep school in Connecticut. He was the thirteenth generation of Loomises since the family settled in America from England. The school had been founded after World War I by a collection of Loomis cousins from funds set aside for it when the first Loomis family member had come from England in 1689. As a direct descendant, Rob had priority and was awarded a scholarship. He was in trouble there almost right away. "My idea of what my time in high school was going to be like was very different from what it was," Rob said. "Some of that was just being naive. I spent a fair amount of time sort of reacting. I smoked marijuana for the first time there and I took LSD once." Rob was frightened and depressed at Loomis. His philosophical differences with the school and his own psychological pain led to increasing difficulty until he finally left after the eleventh grade.

During Vivienne's sixth-grade year her parents made a fateful decision about her education. The sixth grade at Melrose started poorly. The children from the fifth grade told the new ones, "Don't play with Vivienne Loomis. She stinks." "Vivienne began to be so sarcastic and biting I knew we would have to do something with this child," Paulette said. Vivienne and Laurel had been in school only two weeks when Paulette found the school she wanted them to attend. It was a small, private, liberal school founded on Quaker principles. Located in a working-class neighborhood of Cambridge, Massachusetts, the Cambridge Friends School was attended largely by the children of professional people and of Harvard and MIT faculty. It went up to the eighth grade and, fortunately, that year had openings in the sixth and seventh grades for Vivienne and Laurel.

"It was an eye-opener. It made all the difference," Paulette said. "Here was a school that felt as we did, that reinforced all our ideals. Vivienne changed immediately. And then of course there was John May. He was the main teacher for the sixth grade. I think she loved him the day she walked into that school."

John May was a heavyset, sensitive-looking young Californian in his twenties. A picture of him at that time shows him sitting on a school desk, his shirt unbuttoned at the neck, gazing into the camera. His eyes seem humorous, quizzical and undefended. His generous mouth is smiling slightly. A Vietnam draft objector and a Quaker, John had just come to the East to do his alternate service as an x-ray technician in a Boston hospital on the 11:00 A.M. to 8:00 P.M. shift. In the mornings he taught at Cambridge Friends School. A graduate of San Francisco State, he had the warmth and informality one associates with Californians and never felt at ease in the stiffer atmosphere of Boston. He made friends among the CFS faculty but did not feel accepted by them socially, attributing this to the fact that many of the teachers had husbands and wives connected with Harvard or MIT. "I didn't really fit in well in the school world there," John said later. "My easiest friendships were at the hospital."

"The whole sixth grade loved John May," Laurel recalls. "He could make you feel better just by listening. You could tell him anything. I was in seventh grade then, but I remember talking to him once about how smart Vivienne was and how dumb I felt. It really helped. He accepted people for what they were. It boosted your confidence. I think that's what he did for Vivienne too." According to Paulette, John dealt with problems in the open. "He talked with the class about caring for each other. There was no more of this 'stand in the hall' treatment they had at Melrose. Vivienne just blossomed."

John spotted Vivienne and another girl as two sixth-graders who had been outcasts in public school. He was concerned too about a girl who had been physically abused. He undertook to help these children and to increase their self-confidence. He saw Vivienne as a person of special value, sensitive and caring, but who "did not think she was worth much." John praised her work and urged Vivienne to think positively about herself. He would tell her she was beautiful, and offered similar encouragements. "From the start John made Vivienne feel good about herself," Paulette said. Sometimes Vivienne and a new friend would call him at the hospital to talk about themselves and about love in an exploring, idealistic fashion. He could not have anticipated the profound impact all this was to have on Vivienne.

In the spring of her sixth-grade year, several months before she was twelve, Vivienne began to express feelings and ideas about herself in her journal, poems and school compositions. She wondered about life and love, about ideals and ideal persons, and about the possibilities and disappointments of friendships. These writings were inspired by her deepening attachment to John May, and some of them are frankly dedicated to him.

In her journal entry of April 8, 1971, Vivienne wrote,

> Do you understand me? Do you love me? Do you know the things I know? Do you feel the way I feel? . . . I bet nobody knows the things I know or feels the things I feel. Does anyone admire things the way I do? I don't think so, but maybe, no, it couldn't be. Does anyone experience things the way I do? Does anybody take remarks or words the way I do?
>
> Did anybody ever wonder how close they were to their ideal? I do. Does anybody ever wonder how they looked in the eyes of friends? Do people admire me? Does anybody admire me? I hope so. I care what people say to me and what people think about me. I want to set an example that is good. I wish everybody had a healthy brain and I hope I have one anyway. I don't mean to sound stupid or anything, but that's how I really and truely feel. Any way no one will ever read this any way so it's ok.

A week later she wrote, "My idea of an ideal person is someone who is not perfect. Someone who is understanding and sensitive. Someone who has a good sense of humor and can take criticism also. This person would be hardworking and would accept challenges and mistakes for what they were. He would be kind and generous. He would trust. He would see realism and would have ideals. Most of all he would be happy and satisfied with his life."

Both Laurel and Anne felt that Vivienne's idealism was filled with conflict. "She didn't have any perspective about it," Laurel said. "She was always so disappointed when people didn't act the way she thought they ought to." In some ways, Rob felt this too. He thought that family life had not prepared any of them for the outside world.

"I had a lot to learn," Laurel remarked. "For example, we were always told at home that we should be natural, unselfconscious about our bodies. The whole family walked around nude, especially in Maine. But when I got to college I realized that didn't work in the real world. People misunderstood."

All three children began to sense a contradiction in the family attitudes. Even though Paulette and David encouraged them to be comfortable with their bodies, Rob, Laurel and Vivienne all felt that sexuality was forbidden.

"I was acting out a lot," Laurel remembers. "My mother said I was a tease. I told them everything I was doing. Sometimes I think my parents were a little naive. They came from very sheltered lives. My mother's family was all girls, my father's was all boys."

Each of the children reacted to parental concern in a special way. Rob continued to rebel. Laurel became more involved with other people. Vivienne became the family puritan. She had no intimate relationships of her own and she suffered over her brother's and sister's activities.

Her feelings ranged widely. Early in May, she wrote happily to her journal of "that feeling you get when you're in bed at night and you don't know the name. You feel glad that there is no English word to label it with. It's a feeling of love and wonder." But she also began to reflect in her poetry upon existential questions related to her personal identity and being.

> May 12, 1971
> *ME*
> *Where am I?*
> *Would I do better there?*
> *Am I in my place?*
>
> *Does anybody*
> *Move from their mold?*
> *Do people know*
> *Their changes?*
>
> *My place is*
> *My being and*
> *My life is the*
> *Existence of my*
>   *Being.*

During the sixth grade at CFS Vivienne was able for the first time to form a close friendship with another girl. In her diary she wrote of her pleasure in the newfound closeness, and in May she wrote a school composition for John May on the subject of friendship:

> *THE MOST IMPORTANT THING TO ME IS A FRIEND*
>
> To me a friend is the best thing I could have in life. Up until this year I didn't have any true friends. Nobody really cared enough about me to show that they did. If they did. But now things are different.
>
> This year I met someone who does care about me and I care about her an awful lot.... For about a month ... I thought that this person was more interested in someone

else and that I was a tag-along.... I felt like I was a tire on [a] truck and that truck needed four wheels and I was the fifth, unwanted, worn and slightly out of shape.

Anyway, [she] invited me over and I told her that day exactly how I felt. We went out into the field to talk about it.... We talked for a long, long time and by the end we had told each other how much we really loved each other. As we were walking back across the field, she came up and just hugged me and I hugged her back. I ran the rest of the way, there was a new warmth inside me, a very happy warmth, and I wished the whole world knew how really wonderful it is to have someone tell you they love you like that. It's an experience worth living for.

There were times, though, when the relationship was not so joyful. Vivienne felt she had to live up to an expectation of perfection with her new friend and to play a false role in order to do so. "The painful part of playing a role," she wrote in her journal in December, "is that I have the constant feeling that I'm big and clumsy and sort of dense beside someone who is small, precise, brilliant and absolutely perfect. I always feel I'm not meeting her expectations, and she shows a certain weariness at putting up with me.... I don't know how to tell her that I'd rather just be friendly towards her than agree with everything she says."

Looking back, Laurel felt that it was not only Vivienne's intense shyness but also her exacting and unattainable standards that prevented her from having more friends.

Vivienne seemed to change during her sixth-grade year at CFS. Her sarcasm diminished and for the first time she began to be more independent of Laurel in making friends. She also played the flute, took part in dramatic productions, sang in the Melrose Episcopal choir at Christmastime and began to spend more time on writing. During this year Vivienne became freer and happier, but she could still be moody at home. "Sometimes

she was sort of like a court jester," her mother said. "She could
be extremely witty — she could imitate Lily Tomlin — but then
if you happened to see her in a moment when there was nothing much going on — in repose — she really looked sad."

Laurel noticed this, too. "She could be a lot of fun, but she
was basically serious," Laurel commented. "I think people were
really in awe of her. She had so much command of the language,
so much wisdom. People dumped their emotional issues on her
because she was such a good listener."

Vivienne pondered these issues and wrote two poems that reflected her feelings.

1

I looked
I listened
I thought
I reflected

Each person
Each problem
Each wonder
Not neglected

Until I
Understood
These things
I selected.

2

I never become
Too involved
In thinking.
Because I always
Draw back, in an
Unconscious effort
To keep sanity.

Vivienne's tendency to take on the burdens of other family members became evident that spring in relation to Rob. He had gone to Loomis on a scholarship but had fallen in with a group of richer friends. Rob rarely communicated with the family, but reports from the school to Paulette and David seemed ominous to them. He began experimenting with marijuana, mescaline and LSD, according to Paulette, and a former girl friend ran away from home and arrived at Loomis to see him. His mother said he worried, for no medically detectable reason, that he had a bad heart and, according to her, came close to suicide twice. Rob later acknowledged that he had "come up to the edge" of suicide several times. Because of Vivienne's empathy and interest in problem solving, and because David Loomis seemed so overwhelmed in his efforts to deal with Rob, Paulette would turn to her for advice. All of this weighed heavily upon Vivienne. She acknowledged her worries in her journal:

> March 3, 1971
>
> Do you s'pose Rob took LSD more 'n once? I hope not cause there's s'pose to be something hereditary you know, with genes and stuff like that. It certainly was pretty awful when Dad began to cry. I never saw him do it before. I can't blame Mommy for not trusting him but she certainly was too mad to talk to him, that's for sure! Well guess I better just hope and pray.
>
> ... [Rob's] gotten himself into a lot of trouble lately. I wonder what's going to happen in Loomis. I sure hope he isn't going to get in any more trouble. I worry about him a lot. ... The thing is that you don't know what or who to believe. I wish he were safe from all those harmful things. I'll just hope and pray with all my might! Bye!

Vivienne's keen sense of justice showed too in the journal. When Rob was blamed for his former girl friend's running off to see him, Vivienne wrote in her journal:

February 23, 1971

... Robby shouldn't be accused of taking [her] away. She's the one who did it. She should have left a note for her father. He's a crook. He wouldn't even talk it over with her and find out what was wrong. It was him (her father) you know: "Get the Hartford Police to escort her down"! What a nut!

Rob came home from Loomis at the end of May, and Vivienne wrote in her journal:

June 2, 1971

Rob's home for good, well that is, for summer vacation. It's funny the mixed feelings I have, boy they sure are mixed. I mean I love him so much that I can't stand it when he gets hurt and especially when he hurts someone else and that hurts me. Maybe somebody else wouldn't understand what I really mean, but I do so it doesn't matter. He better be OK.

Bye! Vivienne

A month later she put the hurt and frustration she felt about Rob into a poem:

July 2, 1971
About 11:00 P.M.

I've got to help my brother
He needs it real bad.
For me to see him so
Makes my soul feel sad.

I've got a whole lot of love
And I can't keep it in.
Don't know how to give it,
Not even to my kin!

Oh, it's so sad . . . . .
So very sad;
That I don't know how to love.

Her sense of justice and fair play led Vivienne to be used sometimes to settle family disputes. As Rob was packing to return to school following spring vacation, a bag of marijuana fell from his belongings. "I just confiscated it," Paulette said, "and was going to flush it down the toilet." But it turned out to be a purchase Rob had made with his own money. "We had a family conference. Vivienne was the mediator. She said I had no right to take it, that it didn't belong to me. She said it was his even if I didn't approve. In the end I gave it back to him."

Actually, Vivienne did not condone the smoking of marijuana, although she later was to experiment with it a little herself. Laurel recalls that from an early age Vivienne was disapproving and puritanical. She lectured Laurel about drugs and later about her seemingly casual attitudes toward sex.

Although Vivienne's journal does not yet reflect it, there were other concerns that troubled the family. David's ministry was beset with difficulties. There were two churches a block apart. David's church was Universalist; his neighbor's was Unitarian. They had struggled to maintain their individuality despite the fact that their denominations had recently merged. Neither church was thriving. The congregations were considering a united, common church and one of the ministers would have to go. David endured this uncertainty with stoical patience. It was to continue for more than two years, and he would characteristically be the one to make the sacrifice. All three children were aware of their father's unspoken struggle and of his determination to remain fair and charitable.

With the closing of school, Vivienne immediately began to send letters and poems to John May for his critical comment.

June 10, 1971

Dear Mr. May,

I'll bet this is the first letter you've gotten from one of your students since vacation began this afternoon. Rather humorous, don't you think? I have a feeling that you're beginning to think that this letter is a waste of your valuable time. It is.

However, there is a reason (if not a good one) for writing this letter. Just trust me. You see, I wrote this poem tonight (it's about 10:10 P.M. now) that's called "Association with Reality." *I* think it's rather good. But! I would like your opinion. I have copied it over in my Private Paper Book already. (Do you get the feeling I like it?)

I want to know what you think of the structure of the poem. Any words that might happen to be spelled wrong, used incorrectly, etc. (you know, the works). Would you tell me if I used too many descriptive words, please? If you could find the time, I would appreciate it. However! If you feel that this is a general bore, please feel free to insinuate as much in any letter that you might feel up to writing to me. Do feel obligated to answer this letter (unless you're too busy).

Love,

Vivienne

P.S. You'll always be my very, very favorite teacher. (Wish you could teach seventh grade next year.)
P.S.S. Thank you.
P.S.S.S. If you were to like by some strange chance my poem, you can keep it. By the way, about not forgetting that I'm beautiful, how could I forget? No one's ever said that before.

June 10, 1971
Thursday
ASSOCIATION WITH REALITY

It was within my grasping reach.
Groping, wavering, I brushed past
The confined mold of emptiness
And reality, into the elusive world
  of everlasting emotion.

The soft, flowing coolness
Of thought swept through
The regions of my mind.
Rising questions blended together
Into expanding and impending vision;
The piercing, everlasting attempt
To understand the flexibility
  of emotion.

John May replied:

June 22, 1971

Dear Vivienne,

A poem, and probably therefore a poet, is an elusive and wondrous thing. It can provide many functions not the least of which is the poet's exploration of him (her) self. For that reason I often find it difficult to comment "objectively" on a poem written by someone I know. I believe that exploration of self is an extremely valuable thing and don't want to, and shouldn't criticize that search.

Your poem "Association with Reality" is a beautiful piece of writing. It's beautiful for many reasons. It has a sense of mystery. I am not quite sure what you're speaking about, and in poetry, often, this is good. It leads me to wonder. To try to make form out of your words, and I therefore become involved. You are also dealing with an abstract and mysterious thing, a non-concrete reality so the very nature of your subject calls for the abstractness of your text. Now this may seem strange to you that I see your poem as abstract. It may be very real to you. But I think that there are elements which make it more elusive to me such as beginning with "It" when I don't know (I being "reader") the antecedent. Another beauty of your poem is the way that you weave your words. It's true that there are many descriptive words in there and that I have commented about your over use of them at other times. A poet's tool is language. He may do with that as he wishes but it ought to be a conscious use of that tool, so if you choose to use an abundance of descriptive words make certain that it happens consciously and is not used as an easy way out. This brings me to another aspect of poetry in general. The major building blocks of poetry are simile and metaphor (using one thing to represent another). You use these very subtly and naturally, as when you say "the regions of my mind" making your mind into a vast area large enough to embody regions. *Sometimes* "descriptive words" can be a substitute or improved by using metaphor instead. But that doesn't really hold in this poem.

Another beauty of the poem is, of course, you. Your sensitive awareness shows through and that can't be improved upon.

Now for my recommendations. Keep writing as you have said that you are. Don't be too critical now. Use this time to find a style of your own. Satisfy your self. Also read much poetry, not to imitate, or ... make you humble, you've no need for either, but to gain a sense of other people's visions, other people's poetic sense. Might I recommend Emily Dickinson, Robert Frost and Edna St. Vincent Millay. I also enjoy Yevtushenko, Dylan Thomas (talk about word playing) and Theodore Roethke. Don't set someone else's standards on your poetry. Play with it, work with it and enjoy it.

I thank you so much for sharing your writing with me. Please keep it up. I'll try to be more punctual in answer, but I will answer. I'll see you on Saturday.

Shalom —

John May, Mr. May, John

I have just unsealed the letter because I forgot to include a very important thought. The other thing you should do . . . is to continue to live with your perceptors open so that you have the basic material, the only material, for poetry: life.

After receiving this letter, Vivienne posed a question in her journal: "Perhaps all my poems will be abstract because nobody feels the things that I write, and therefore having them read my poems is like taking them through fairyland. But I also think it better for them to have the experience of reading it than not. Don't you?"

Because it would have betrayed her feelings too clearly, Vivienne did not send John May her most intimate poem of this period. She did, however, read it to her family.

June 16, 1971
TAKE MY HAND
Take my hand in your hand
And walk me through a lifetime.
Walk me over a bridge of
observation.
With me wade through a pool of
knowledge.
Together we would climb through
a tree of communication.

Over we would walk a mountain of
discovery.
Then walk me over a field of
honesty.
Walk me down a silent path of
thought.
And at the end of our walk,
we will find ourselves in a
valley of friends.
Together we will understand
a lifetime of love.
So —
Take my hand in yours
and walk me through a
lifetime.

Analyzing her poem, she confided to her journal ("My Private Paper Book") her special conception of love. She reiterated her uncompromising investment in the ideal and made her first reference to disappointment and depression.

June 22, 1971
A STEP INTO THE LAND OF THOUGHT

I'm glad I could write "Take My Hand in Yours" because I can't send it to Mr. May because I'm afraid he wouldn't get the real true meaning I intended him to get. You know. About the love. When I read it to my family, they thought I meant "we" would love each other, instead of what I meant, which was that I would love the people in the valley of friends and the people in the valley of friends would love me. I don't want this to be a case of misunderstand. I think I meant to put in a good amount of security along with everything else. I hope whoever reads my poems will get as much out of it as I put into it. I don't love life, I just love the little bit of life that touches my ideal one. It's my ideal life I love and try to live and introduce into the lives of others. All I can do is hold my stand and not give up until I've accomplished what I want to and not give up or out with exhaustion or with depression and disappointment. I just won't. I'll just stick with it. I will, I will. No matter how hopeless it seems right now. I'll be persistent.

Goodbye.

P.S. Don't forget that two of Mr. May's nicknames are Handsome and Sugarbug. I am writing them here for later reference.

The summer of 1971 was a happy one for Vivienne, but it was her relationship to John May that sustained her. She was not yet twelve but her mother felt that Vivienne was truly in love. A friend of Vivienne's thought so too, Paulette recalls. "Once Vivienne told me that this child said to her, 'If Mary [John's girl friend] wasn't the one he loved, you'd want him for yourself, wouldn't you?' Well, Vivienne was so indignant. She swore up and down it wasn't true. But imagine — Vivienne — so hungry for acceptance and this warm, caring young man!"

John knew that he was important to Vivienne, but it wasn't until after her death that he realized what a critical role he played for her. The letters he received that summer were a mixture of ordinary news, teasing and some sharing of her deepest thoughts. But it was in her journal, in poems and notes, that her most profound and intimate searchings occurred. Most of these did not come to light until after her death. At times she would address the journal as if it were a personal friend:

> July 8, 1971
> *My feelings mingle with questions*
> *That I don't know*
> *How to answer.*

What I believe intertwines
With what I feel,
And still I don't know
How to answer.

When I attempt to interpret
What I believe ideally into real life,
Sometimes I get really lost
In a maze,
And still I don't know
How to answer.

Once I went way down deep,
To see if I could answer
My understanding of Love.
I found a warm soft glow ...
But still I don't know
How to answer.

In a peaceful world of thought,
I let go of the ropes
That kept me from falling.
And I fell, I fell into a world
Where I can understand.
And sometimes, just sometimes,
I know .....
How to answer.

John and his girl friend were invited for dinner and Vivienne remarked upon the occasion in her journal.

July 21, 1971

Mr. May came over with Mary on Sunday the 18th for supper. Originally he was going to come about one, but he finally got here around 5:30. I wonder if people will like me as much as they do John.

It's funny, I didn't think Mr. May would understand my love, but he does and that's what I've been hoping all along. It's too good to be true. I'm really very, very happy. I guess that's why I like him so much. I mean, he knows just how I want to be treated most of the time, almost all of it. He's the only one who is like that with me; sincere, trusting, honest and loving. I love him for that. Really.

> Bye, signed Me

In late July the Loomis family went to their summer cottage in Maine, the "Little Brown Jug." It was a relaxed family time and Vivienne and Laurel enjoyed the people and the life there. Vivienne wrote a newsy, cheerful letter to John May. At the very end she added:

Now I have something to tell you which I've been meaning to tell you every time I have called you. (Sigh) But now I *will* tell you. I want to say how grateful I am for *everything* you have given me this year. You've made such an influence on me that it is [a] good thing you're who you are. I don't know how to express my gratitude, other than being the happy, satisfied person I am.

> Joy,
>
> *Viv*

On August 13 Vivienne received a letter from John May wishing her a happy birthday, but she had evidently talked to him on the phone too.

> August 13, 1971

Dear John,
Hey John —
That was really nice of you to tell me that I was beautiful. Sometimes..... when I really feel out, I think to

myself: "I'm no good. I'm not slender, I don't smile a lot, I'm not outgoing, I'm not even halfway "pretty"! But then I remember what you said about my being beautiful inside and out! I bet you figured that since I value everything you say, that if you said that, I would really believe it and would be more certain of myself. But what it's done is to make me happy for days on end — thinking of how you — John May — thought I was beautiful! And I guess I'm beginning to really believe it!

On her birthday she wrote again ("at 2:30 P.M. . . . the exact time I was born"), confiding her worries about the new teachers she would have at school, and she continued:

> . . . Oh! It's getting rough and I can hear the bell buoy clanging in the distance. That's what I like about The Little Brown Jug. . . . I thought one of the lobsters was climbing out of his pan. Oh, yes. I'm having lobster for dinner. Dieter's Delight I call it. Actually, I'm not dieting any more, until I get back to school, anyway. I figure, all this exercise and three good meals a day (no snacks) and I'll be O.K. I won't say I've lost, but I haven't gained.
>
> Well thanks for writing. Thank you very much for writing and "I'm glad you were born" and I think "you're neat" too.

Toward the end of August Vivienne wrote John about her summer activities and her delight in being in his drama class. She mentioned too the changes she had noticed in herself and commented that she had overcome her shyness to attend a square dance for "people who are thirteen years of age or older."

> . . . I just couldn't stand the idea of being so alone here, so I decided I would go along and draw in the back of the kitchen (at the Yacht Club, of course). But Dad danced

one dance with me anyway. In the end I danced *seven* dances (including Dad's), all of which I was asked!!! (Don't forget this was thirteen and older!) One guy (who danced three dances with me) got me drinks and walked me to the door at the very end! Two other people asked me and I was very, very surprised! Mostly because they were all over seventeen, I'd say. The square dances were fairly difficult in themselves. But all these "L-M-N Lefts," "Grand Right and Lefts," "Left girl high — Right girl lows" and "Side ladies chain across" and "Chain back homes" didn't worry me in the least, and if I do say so myself, I did quite well! Well, it was exciting for me, because I've never, never been asked by a boy before in my life! They swung me around and we laughed and got all hot and happy. (If they just knew I had only just turned twelve!) ... Never before in my life have I laughed and joked with someone I never saw before! I've changed.

Vivienne faced her seventh-grade year with greater self-confidence. She and Laurel were looking forward to Cambridge Friends School. While John May would not be Vivienne's classroom teacher, he was still on the faculty and conducted special seminars that Vivienne could join. Her classroom teacher that year was Mike Nelson. Her first composition for him described her feelings about school:

September 25, 1971

SCHOOL

For me school is a place for being myself, meaning if you are acquainted with me, there is a perfect chance of your knowing ME. Not "Vivienne Loomis," ME! You see I haven't put up a fake person for you to know; I've been completely Me.

And that's the really neat thing about school. Even at

home I'm not as much myself as at school. I think the reason is that when I first came to Friends everybody was their own self and it was extremely hard (but really in my case impossible) for me to be only the very surface of my soul, or, for that matter, my name. And so, after eleven years, I finally learned how to live with myself as well as with other people.

Later in the fall, Vivienne wrote about her respect and concern for the earth:

November 5, 1971
WHAT I THINK WE OWE TO THE EARTH

I think that perhaps we owe the earth respect. I mean this in the sense that either we are a part of the earth's civilization, or the earth is a part of our civilization. It's awfully hard for me to tell which exists right now.

If we had respect for this earth (not "our" earth), maybe we wouldn't think we had the right to pollute and destroy it.

Also, I think we should be grateful for everything the earth has given us: food, a place to live, sources for work and pleasure, a place for civilization to occur.

Some people have said to me, "If you feel so strongly about this, why don't you go live in a commune and stop polluting yourself? Stop wearing watches. Why don't you stop using dishwashers?" And my only answer is, "What good will it do me (or anything) if you don't come live on it too?" But would you?

That year Vivienne wrote an assertive poem sharply defining herself.

I am the youngest in my family
I am one out of twenty in the seventh grade.

I am the minister's daughter.
I am a pretender of moods.
I am a New Englander.
I am a person who plays the flute.
I am very polite.
I am a girl
I am me — because everyone is "me" inside
everything else

While Vivienne was certainly a New Englander, John May was definitely a Californian and had never expected to stay in the East. In the late fall she learned for the first time that he was planning to return to the West Coast after the following year. The impact of this news on Vivienne was profound. The next journal entry contains the first hint of suicide.

November 9, 1971

I wish Mr. May wouldn't go next year. And I wish Dad and Mummy wouldn't keep reminding me that he is.

A weaker, more immediate wish is that Mr. May would invite us to dinner like he said he would.

An impossible wish, though strongest, is that he would invite *me* (alone). Because I love him.

He is going to leave me.

Forever????

He's going to leave me behind as he goes on his merry way. But if he leaves me what way will I have to go? Why won't he stay? When will I die? It seems like I ought to die now while the going's good. While life has still got some joy. That joy will be gone in a year. Maybe I will be too — oh, ah, silver tears appearing now. I'm crying, ain't I?

Although she tried to reach out to other teachers, Jeff Lob and Mike Nelson, she anticipated the loss of John May with grief and anger. She nicknamed him "the Turtle," and wrote a satiric story in French about a turtle who sometimes liked to stay in his shell.

There were troubles at home too. Rob was floundering in his junior year at Loomis School. He failed a required algebra course and his friends, teachers and dorm parents were worried about him. Laurel, now fourteen, was becoming more adventurous and was experimenting sexually.

Later Anne Tucker, a friend, recalled conversations with Vivienne about Laurel. "She was really upset that Laurel would do such a thing, but she was even more upset that Laurel had lied to her. For Vivienne *that* was the worst thing. She couldn't forgive it. At first, before I really knew Laurel, I hated her because of what Vivienne told me. But later I understood. I could see why Laurel tried to keep things smooth."

Vivienne's outrage about Laurel accompanied her own search for a personal code. A letter she and a friend composed for John May reveals something of her inner debate about the nature of love.

[Undated — probably winter 1971–72]

Dear Mr. May,

What we really wanted to tell you on the phone is that we love you. Not "love" love, but admiration and consideration and friendship love. But it's kind of hard to say it on the phone.

We were talking about you in the field. We were saying that if you really love someone, you should be able to tell that person without being ashamed. That's why we're telling you.

We were saying that the world needs more love, and it's terrible to be ashamed of something wonderful like love, and not be ashamed of something terrible like hate. Also I agree with Vivienne and she agrees with me.

Love...

P.S. We both think that the world should be able to say these things without feeling that people will laugh and say it's stupid.
P.S.S. Ditto

What [we] were talking [about], or rather trying to talk about was that we love you. And the more we talked about it, the more we really felt the need to express it. By hugging you. Do you understand?

But then, when we were with you, well, to me everything began to sound stupid. I guess this is because of the little things like when you wrote me a letter you said something like "to those who love you or just *know* you" and when you said, "I knew you *liked* me a lot!" I mean, even though you really did realize that it was love I was talking about, you might not understand, since it seems as though you may like me, but you probably don't *love* me. And *I* do love you, so you *might* not understand. But I hope that someday I'm loved as much as you are.

Love,

Vivienne

P.S. When I finished talking to you tonight, I walked into the dining room and cried. Why??

John May replied:

Vivienne

I wanted to thank you for your comment to me on the phone. I realize how hard it is to tell someone what you told me, but it really made me feel super good. So often people don't tell each other of the good things. So thank you! It goes without saying that I admire you both very much also.

Shalom

Vivienne was also curious about sex and intimacy and tested her mother. Once when she was twelve Vivienne said out of the blue, "Mummy, when I'm eighteen you'll think it's all right for me to come home with a boyfriend and to sleep with him in our house." Paulette thought about this for a while and said, "I don't think I'm going to change that much."

David was having an upsetting time too. He had put his name into the national office to seek another church, but the officials took over a year to offer him a new assignment. There were members of the Melrose congregation who disapproved of the Loomis family. "They were nasty and gossipy," Paulette remarked. "There was this pompous official. For four weeks straight he brought board members to our house. They stayed from ten at night until two in the morning sometimes. For one thing they conducted a survey of the congregation asking for complaints, so of course they got them. They said I was a terrible housekeeper and David had poor eyesight. Here is a typical example: When we moved into the house the garage door was rusted open. It wouldn't budge. It looked disorderly, I guess, full of bikes and garden tools. Once when the church Couples Club met, I asked all the men to help me close that garage door. They couldn't do it." The open garage door turned out to be an item on the complaint list. "They even cut David's salary because they said I had a job at the library. I'm sure the girls must have heard all of this." In a poem Vivienne wrote later she refers to these "bloody knives."

TO MY FATHER

To understand
The common crowds and bloody knives
And keep your faith
In smallest puppies
And simple God.

You give away smiles
Over faded flowers
Give your life
And take it in
Under no pretext.

Weigh unscientifically
The rays of sun, and admit
That you are blinded
In all of that
White-hot energy.

Away from the sun,
You recognize the sequin glitter
And shout it from the roof
(You have woken up
The sleepiest birds)

... Admit it all ...
To understand
The common crowds and bloody knives
And keep your faith
In smallest puppies
And simple God.

Although David Loomis had trouble understanding his daughter, he always felt there was a close bond between them. He thought later that Vivienne, who regularly came to church services, could not have helped being affected by his struggles.

David remained reasonable in spite of the community's attacks, but the situation was frustrating for Paulette and painful to the children. "I think Dad sacrificed himself for the sake of the church," Rob remarked later. "He didn't want to cause controversy for the other minister or hurt either church. I think Vivienne worried about Dad, bearing all of these problems."

As the new year began, Vivienne pondered her place in the world and the nature of her imperfections. She recorded her deliberations in the journal.

January 4, 1972
NOTHING TO BE MENTIONED

I have spent quite a lengthy time pondering upon (poetic, is it not?) the actions of people (based, actually, on me).

I observe that when I don't want to be noticed, I wear dark clothes so that I won't stand out. . . .

I observe too, that when one does want to be noticed, he either acts extremely witty, behaves fairly loudly, or in some cases, unnaturally silently.

In making friends I notice that some people immediately assume that you are their special friend. I also notice that more often than not other people do not appreciate and are more apt to resent this. So far, I have found that the best way to gain a friend is to respect (and I will admit, very highly in my case) the person and his values.

Also I find that the best way to alienate somebody (in my case) is to be certain within yourself that YOU are right. I myself stay on the safe side and keep it firmly in my mind that the other guy is always of superior intelligence. However, everyone knows that I have alienated people. But that comes with the imperfect being that I am. And of course you must not be offended by the sense of "I-know-it-allness" . . .

John May taught two seminars, "God" and "Peace," discussion classes that included guest speakers. Vivienne's disillusion with the Melrose church and her growing personal despair led her to take these subjects especially seriously.

April 12, 1972

SEMINAR
"GOD"

I really want to believe in something, but like many others, I don't know what, yet. I thought that going to this seminar might give me an answer, and while it didn't do that, it certainly made me think about things I never thought about before. The reason I didn't talk much was because I was really listening.

The people who impressed me to the greatest extent were, I think, the people from Transcendental Meditation [she tried it herself, but wrote in her journal that it hurt her back], the Jesus People Movement and the Baha'i Faith. . . .

The Baha'i Faith impressed me . . . in the principle of believing, but really fascinated me as far as their ideas of peace and converting the world to the Baha'i Faith. I personally feel that this is wrong because who is to say that the Baha'i Faith is "right" for the *world?* Maybe Judaism is "right." I'm sure everyone who strongly believes in his religion feels that it is right, but if all these people tried to convert the world there would be a World Religious War, and that is not peace. I feel (perhaps more strongly than anything else) that religious beliefs are things to introduce to people, but not things you push on them as right. I believe that no religion is right for every individual.

All ways, I believe, of looking at "God" are believable and should be respected.

Of the Peace seminar, Vivienne wrote:

The seminar itself was good, I think. I believe that the point of appreciating people was to get you to see the good things in other people, the result, perhaps of being at peace or more at peace with others. I think "news and goods" was an attempt to make you see what was good in your life and perhaps be more at peace with yourself. (If this is true I think it failed to reach me, because I've never been more depressed in my life. Sorry I can't say it has nothing to do with this seminar. I think I'm developing a strong inferiority complex.)

The "inferiority complex" haunted the rest of Vivienne's short life. Recognizing the egocentric basis of her growing depression, Vivienne captured this insight in a poem written in February.

> ### PATTERNS OF MY LIFETIME
> *Crossing over, then down*
> *Falling over, then under:*
> *Down through egotistical*
> *Patterns made in my lifetime.*
>
> *Emotional depression*
> *Existing, at first unobserved:*
> *An old forgotten sword . . .*
> *Suddenly glistening and sharp!*
>
> *Eternal hope alternating*
> *From blind, whimsical dependence*
> *To strong, resounding salvation:*
> *A bright candle in the night.*
>
> *Sentiment weaving its way*
> *Through hope in depression,*

> *Depression in hope:*
> *An amazing grace in itself.*
>
> *Crossing over, then down.*
> *Falling over, then under:*
> *Down through egotistical*
> *Patterns made in my lifetime.*

Vivienne struggled to form strong ties with her new seventh-grade teachers, Jeff Lob and Mike Nelson, but she did not feel that she mattered to them in the way she did to John May. "Jeff misunderstood us today," she wrote in her journal at the end of March. "Sometimes I don't know if he cares at all about me. He does but he doesn't show it. Maybe he doesn't care about me but about French. . . . I wish he really liked me." She continued to try to engage Jeff and, with a friend's help, began to deny her grief at John May's approaching departure.

April 3, 1972

Today I (and ———) talked to Jeff Lob and I have really decided to get rid of as much shell as possible. I guess there really is a person in there after all. I think I have gotten to the point where I genuinely *like* him. (But I think I like Mr. Nelson more.)

April 4, 1972

I realize that I don't mind Mr. May going to California any more, it doesn't make any difference to me. I agree with [my friend] when she says that never showing anger, etc. is a shell in itself. Boy, does Mr. May have a shell.

I am so glad that [my friend] feels like me sometimes, too. Boy, what a relief!!

John May sensed Vivienne's unhappiness. Her journal records his efforts to boost her confidence and reveals how much she still relied upon him to sustain her self-regard.

April 13, 1972

Today John May came and talked to me in the hall. He sort of embarrassed me, but he made me feel good because he saw himself in me. Charlene [the music director] kept on yelling for him but he kept on talking.

You see, I wasn't feeling so hot about myself and he told me that I was beautiful, gentle and sensitive. At the end he said, "I love it when that one cheek blushed." I'm, so he told me, to go to him every day and tell him something good about myself or he would. He was nice, I had the feeling that it wasn't just his role as "counselor," but that he really cared.

April 25, 1972

... During typing Mr. May opened the door and asked to see me. I felt very important. He said he owed me two things. Then he told [me] two good things about [myself].

Despite John May's support, Vivienne felt more despair the next month about the separations and losses ahead.

May 5, 1972

Today was about the worst day of this year. The fact that I've got a really sore throat doesn't help because I have to keep quiet and being quiet brings on depression for me. I don't think anyone really likes me. I feel like they've all been pretending all year. I feel like crying.

May 9, 1972

Jeff Lob is not going to come back next year. That is too bad. I was sort of counting on him to be a teacher I would know next year. Boy, am I glad Charlene's going to be here! Am I going to be lonely next year!

May 11, 1972

... Why do I have to like the people that are with me the shortest time in my life? Sometimes I think it's not worth the let-down in the end.

The same day Vivienne wrote Rob a newsy letter describing a performance in a Harvard church that Cambridge Friends School students sang in. Only the last few lines give a hint of what she was going through:

... *Anyway*, the shocking thing was that as I started walking, I suddenly realized that this church was actually *jammed!* I've never seen a full church before! (Don't tell Dad I said that!) Well, anyway, it was really fun.

There are three teachers that I am very close to in this school: Jeff Lob, John May, Mike Nelson. None of them are going to be here next year. I always seem to get attached to the people [who] leave me the soonest in life. Why?!

In her May 15 journal entry, Vivienne was again worried about John May's feelings for her. "Today was O.K. I really don't think Mr. May cares about me." Three days later she was still unsure: "Mr. May mentioned how much he liked 'us,' but I still feel no more than the bad half of it. I don't know why."

David's twenty-fifth Harvard reunion came up that spring. The whole family was planning to go. Vivienne had been looking forward to it, but two events upset her. Rob and Laurel smoked marijuana at the reunion and Paulette appeared in a new outfit. "It was an outrageous dress," Laurel remembers, "and she wore all this makeup. Vivienne was shocked." Experiences like these seemed to drive Vivienne back into herself and increase her loneliness. Her feelings of isolation show in the next poem she wrote.

> *My mind is like a cool shady nook,*
> *A place where I can retreat*
> *Or hide*
> *When I need to be alone.*
> *You cannot push your way in*
> *Shove your way in*
> *Force your way in.*
> *You can't come in unless I invite you.*
> *But if I do*
> *You can come in.*

When Rob returned from Loomis School that spring, it was apparent he had barely managed to get through the year. The school was not planning to ask him back, but Rob withdrew before this became official. Laurel graduated from Cambridge Friends that same June. Both Laurel and Rob were scheduled to attend another private school, in Waltham, Massachusetts — Rob for his senior year, Laurel for ninth grade. Vivienne was to feel a deepening loneliness at Cambridge Friends School. The year marked an estrangement from friends there and her first real separation from Laurel.

Vivienne looked forward to the family vacation in Maine, but wrote of her loneliness beforehand in a letter to John May she never mailed.

Sunday evening, 9:55 P.M.
July 2, 1972

Dear Mr. May (Or ... the Tender Tardy Turtle),

... You do realize that you promised to come to Maine don't you? 'cause you better start making arrangements!! Also here is a work of art (?!) that I'll bet you haven't got time to read and aren't the least interested in — so here it is! (Big Deal!) Oh! by the way, I *just* finished writing it, so there's probably lots I should have changed but haven't. Here goes!

> *I saw your image clearly*
> *I really can't complain*
> *But now you're smeared*
> *Completely through my window pane.*
>
> *The frost glazed over and*
> *I really can't explain*
> *Why I wait for season's changes*
> *To unsmear my window pane.*
>
> *And your shrouded figures*
> *Fade so quickly*
> *Into dust*
> *Gathered in these past years*
> *Half dissolving*
> *Into my own tears.*

I am fully aware of your pressive schedule, but do you think you could squeeze in some time to write me? Can I talk to [you] just for a sec? I wasn't going to write this because it sounds so dumb, but there's a rumor in my mind that's being spread that says you don't much care for me any more. My problem is that I believe it whether it's true or not.

I just read that over, and I feel like ripping up this whole letter, it's so trashy and stupid (shitty would describe it better), but I can't afford to waste the stationary. I don't know what you think of me but for the rest of this letter I'm going to pretend that it's like it used to be.

I'm listening to James Taylor singing "You Got a Friend" on the radio, and somehow I wish it weren't just a song. You have no idea what the disappearance of *all* your friends including your sister (who is in Maine) plus a reunion that is over can do to you. I don't think I've ever been so lonely in my life!!! Now even the song is over and I haven't even got that! I don't think I'm the "student with both feet on the ground" (as someone put it) any more: I think [I'm] sinking into the mud.

Sorry to be so gloomy. I apologize. This *is* such a bore. Write to me soon please?

Love, Vivienne (Loomis)

P.S. *If* you really do come to Maine and it *happens* to be anywhere around the *14th* of August, you *could* always make me something.

P.S.S. *Please* write! ...

P.S.S.S. Do you realize that you are the only person whose present address I know? (Who I can't call.) Well, you are!

John did come to Maine — for three days. Laurel and Vivienne spent the preceding two weeks inventing practical jokes for his visit. Some of the more elaborate pranks (for example, a wolf face they planned to create to appear at his window, complete with howls) were never carried out, but the girls did make green eggs and ham for breakfast (patterned on a Dr. Seuss book) and substituted salt for sugar in the morning coffee. John's stay was short and Paulette felt that Vivienne was disappointed. Her poetry at the time expresses inner storm and the destruction of her hopes and dreams.

> *Leaves*
> *That drip*
> *From branches;*
> *The sunshine flowers*
> *That catch their shade.*
> *I was young then,*
> *And didn't know.*

Of frost
That bites
So cruelly
At filtered
Shafts
Of sunlit flowers
Dying quietly . . .

That
Summer breezes
Turn to
Whipping winds
That tear
Your cries
In two.

That the earth
Below
A river
Flowing steadily
A young boy humming
Up in a tree
Alongside

Might
One day
Tremble hard
To draw
Crashing down
These things
Into the ground.

That beautiful waves
Rolling softly in
On the tide
Should one day
Turn in stormy anger
Under
A darkened sky;

To thrash out
At a passing ship,
To hold it there
In clenched fists,

> *To smash it there*
> *Into a shattered wreck*
> *Of hopeless dreams ...*
>
> *... I was young then,*
> *And didn't know ...*

For Vivienne that fall, as she began the eighth grade, Cambridge Friends School was a changed place. Laurel had graduated, John May would be leaving during the winter, and two other teachers she had cared about were gone. For the first time school itself seemed "like a drag" to her. To John May she seemed a bit more cynical, more closed off. As usual, Vivienne turned to her journal to confide her loneliness and longings.

September 26, 1972

Lots of the time I find myself wishing that the teachers from last year were still here. It makes you very lonely without them. It seems like I'm lonely a lot of the time, which [is] too much of the time. I keep on telling myself that I don't have to be, but what it takes is not being lonely (which is harder than the saying).

October 11, 1972

School is a real drag. It's the same every day; no better, no worse. Nothing happens. In one way more needs to happen (that's exciting, I mean), and in another way, I need the time to catch up and get ahead in my homework. There's no incentive any more.

Also, I need a friend. Not just someone to hang out with but a real friend. It's hard as hell not having a really good one.

Events in the outside world further troubled Vivienne. She was worried about Watergate, prison reform, and events in the daily news that involved suffering that human beings caused one another.

These are the final two paragraphs of an English paper on corruption in the government written on October 30, 1972:

THE WHITE HOUSE PLUMBERS

I could go on forever, but to spare you, I won't. The point is that (as I see it) an amazing amount of highly immoral and immature activities are being carried out in our government. Whether Nixon has been in on them or not, it is inexcusable on his part. For if he *does* know about these things (which I'm convinced he does), and hasn't done anything about it, then he is unfit to serve (from my point of view), and if he *doesn't* know what's going on beneath him, then I say he doesn't have control — and if you don't have control, you shouldn't have the position of President of the United States. If I could vote, this would be one of the very highest considerations that I would take into account.

I don't see how a Senator could do anything about what is done so secretly inside a little core of people. However, if I ever were a Senator, I would try to bring together a massive amount of people in revolt of this system. Ultimately, to bring about changes with justified actions for the good of the people and not just *one man*. For power and greed are the source of all evil.

In November, a prisoner, as part of a special school program, described daily life in jail. Vivienne commented in her journal.

Wasn't that horrible about the prisons? A man doesn't have any rights or respect or anything! I knew that it was *really* bad in the prisons, but I didn't know it was that bad. I guess the general public really doesn't know because they are told stories that they like to hear about, and *not* the truth. What should I do?!

Two poems, written in the depth of night, described the storm and cold within her.

> SUNDAY MORNING: 1:00 A.M.
> *Knocking, clanking . . .*
> *A shattering smash*
> *As a branch falls against the house,*
> *Then down onto the hardened ground.*
>
> *The wind rushing past:*
> *No time to stop and chat . . .*
> *Racing faster now,*
> *Leaving a trail of broken branches*
> *And fallen trees behind.*
>
> *And now it comes whipping through again.*
> *Taking your breath away from you*
> *(To gather more for its own strength.)*
>
> *To smash through*
> *In the dead of night.*
>   November 17, 1972

> *Not knowing where to go next*
> *With whom to pour your heart*
> *When there is really no one.*
>
> *And where would you say the*
> *Moon lies*
> *With winter on its way?*
> *Both walls are cold,*
> *Unblinking off-white.*

> *Teach me how*
> *To defend my needs*
> *From that which is*
> *Life.*
> *...I ask you*
> *What now?*

Vivienne faced an important decision in December. Where should she go to school after her spring graduation from Cambridge Friends? Laurel wanted to change schools too. Rob would be going to college. Both Laurel and Vivienne decided to apply to the Cambridge School of Weston, Massachusetts, a progressive, innovative high school, about to embark on a new "module" system of learning, the intensive study of one or two subjects at a time. Both girls were attracted by the school's emphasis on the arts and its reputation for close faculty-student relations.

On her application form, Vivienne wrote of her love for poetry. "This is sometimes very hard, like gravel in a deep wound, because the world is often harsh, but poetry is extremely beautiful, far more beautiful than the world is harsh." For a question that asked her to discuss a book she found exciting, Vivienne wrote on *The Accident* by Elie Wiesel:

> Personally, I find this to be an especially interesting subject, as I am drawn to death and all that is unknown about it. . . .
>
> I have come to consider *death* an emotional, deep and poetical fact of life. . . .
>
> Like the man in the book, this stage in my life is one of depression. But unlike the man in the book, I have learned to live for Spring. I have taken the other road; I have chosen life. . . .

I look forward to dying, but I will live my life to the fullest first. Death will befall me; I will not befall death.

In spite of this positive statement, Vivienne's poetry spoke of her emptiness and discouragement. Shortly after sending in her application she wrote this poem:

> *And then*
> *There are times*
> *When I have nothing*
> *To look forward to*
> *In life*
> *At all.*
> *Like now.*

The next day she wrote a more extended discussion of *The Accident* that is more ominous:

December 12, 1972

ENGLISH

OVERDUE BOOK REPORT

The Accident has triggered a definite reaction from me on the subject of death. In the first place, reading the book made me realize that *now*, if someone should live for death or in it willingly, I would understand them perfectly.

To live in a world where everything is surface, irrelevant and bitter, . . . it is easy to turn to death which is not only just another escape, but also sacred and true. I say true because truth is not always that easy to come by in life.

I have often thought of death as a retreat, myself, but somehow I always have had the guts to find the truth in life, along with the bitter. I think that the main character in the story just plain wasn't strong enough to go past

all the bitterness and find all the things he missed before:
Love and comfort. Joy and peace. True meaning.

I believe that the difference between life and death (by
will) is having the strength to stand up (again?).

(I can't write any more on this!)

In the beginning months of 1973 no one close to Vivienne
would have thought it was to be the last year of her life. On
the whole, she seemed more independent and cheerful. "I was
really surprised," her father commented later. "She arranged
things for herself — even did a lot more things without Laurel." Some journal entries record lively teenage escapades that
often delighted Vivienne, a busy singing schedule in choirs,
and a production of *Godspell* in which she had a small part.
But her poetry in this period and the journal entries and letters
beginning in April tell of loneliness and deepening despair. No
one in her family ever saw this writing; in fact, personal privacy was regarded as sacred among all the Loomises. Vivienne
said, "Mommy, that is my private stuff and don't read it." "I
never saw anything she wrote until after she died," Paulette
said. "Had I been the kind of mother who goes up and reads
it anyway, I might have gotten very tense and insisted that she
have counseling and saved her life."

The first (undated) journal entry of that year begins with a
French verb. The few words capture what is to come.

perdre — to lose
perdrai

I share with you my life. You must tell me where it
leads to now. The paths confuse me so much. Perhaps
you will guide me?

I believe that I will lose my life because you are not
here. I imagine you. If you are to lead me, it will be
down imaginary paths. Ah, our imaginary life! But I have

let go of the true one. All that is lost is everything. We still have nothing left just for ourselves.

Two poems that followed speak of her emptiness, terror, and longing for closeness.

1

You reach for a smile
But there is no one there
To reflect it.
You are utterly and absolutely
Alone.

Will there never be a hand
To grasp at yours within the mirror?
Will there never be an arm
To hold you tight amidst the terror?

The oddly methodical
Frenzy builds;
The terror of the moon is about you.
But it closes in
Only to stop and pause
And wonder why an arm lies empty.

Grasping hands flinch
In the pale, cool light of the moon.
And empty arms encompass it;
Blinding you for a moment.

But you will see
As you hold up your mirror
That it is only the empty sun
Which you have found.

You are alone.

2

Life is a thing to be experienced
    or is it?
A meaningless existence known to me
    or is it?
A thing of beauty to be so cherished
    or is it?
A thing not worth living tomorrow for
    or is it?
A thing that you take as
Each day appears.

A few days later Vivienne wrote a poem that both Laurel and Paulette felt afterward was written to them.

TO ONE ONCE CLOSE
Why your crazy
Mixed up mind?
Silly decisions,
Vital mistakes

Time to spare
Your unique person
A mere ant
On the earth

Yet you walk still
Spread your disease
Infect the others
Infect yourself.

I can't help you:
You won't understand
The sphere of your mind
Does not include mine.

> You have killed so much
> Joy, and saved your own
> But you have lost your
> Proportion; so your mind.
>
> Never knowing
> What's in my mind
> Yet I know exactly
> What's in yours.
>
> Why your crazy
> Mixed up mind?
> Silly decisions
> Vital mistakes?
>
> Give up and surrender
> That which is not yours
> And is unremarkable.
>
> Realize that you are better
> And will outlive it all
> One hundred times again.
>
> And keep yourself steady
> Because once you were close
> And could appreciate
> > The slightest thing
> > That you could hold on to.
>
> Lose your affection
> For no importance
> And meaningless gifts
> (That were thrown
> For you to catch.)
>
> Give up and surrender.

She considered a similar theme, in a lighter vein, revealing her precocious insight into human egocentrism.

February 4, 1973

ENGLISH
FABLE

ON VANITY

Once upon a time there lived a ravishing princess named Prunelda. Prunelda was an extremely vain creature and very hard to please. She dabbled in the arts a bit, but only to the extent of painting self-portraits. She spent days on end in her rooms, which consisted almost solely of mirrors, and this caused her father, King Kong, to indulge in quite a bit of worrying. Prunelda had to get married off soon, or he'd never be rid of her.

Well, not far off in a near-by kingdom lived a dazzling prince named Prince Hector. He, too, was vain and hard to please. One of the most vain things about him was the fact that he wore mirror glasses — the wrong way 'round. Prince Hector did this because he liked to gaze into his eyes and marvel at their beauty. Hector had heard stories of Prunelda and her room of mirrors, and so he decided that he must definitely marry her. This meant that he would be allowed to frequent her rooms as often as he wished, and *that* meant that he would be able to gaze at himself as frequently as he wished by merely looking into her mirrors.

And so he set about his task. He thought that the best technique would be to go and show Prunelda what a *dazzling* beauty he was. Surely *she* would know true beauty when she saw it. Well, he got an appointment with her for 3:00 Tuesday in her room of mirrors.

At 3:50 Tuesday afternoon, Prunelda and Hector could be found sitting back to back gazing into the mirrors, entranced in themselves. Soon the compliments came gushing out for themselves: "Splendid! ... Magnificent! ... Ah!!"

Each thought that the other's compliments were for himself and so they took a great liking to each other (not that they ever actually saw each other!).

King Kong knew a sure thing when he saw one, and so he had them married right away. Hector and Prunelda spent many fun-filled years staring into mirrors and what turned out to be flattering each other. So *everyone* lived happily ever after.

The moral to this story is that if you're extremely vain, what you don't know can only help you.

Long journal entries in late March and early April have a playful tone, rare in Vivienne's writings although not, according to Laurel, so unusual for her generally. She had missed school to spend a Monday to Friday with Laurel and her father in Maine, which was followed by "the best week-end that I have had in ages." At thirteen and a half, Vivienne's growing interest in sex has a naughty-younger-sister, prankish and make-believe quality.

March 25, 1973
9:50 P.M. Sunday
Oh, yes! Friday night we had a great pillow fight in Rob's room. It was a fight between Susan, Rob, Eddy, Laurel and me.

... The thing was that we turned out the lights so that you couldn't see where anybody was and pretty soon Rob and Susan were down. That left two bodies to walk and fall over. In the condition I was in, I only needed a good stiff blow, and you know like on those cartoons, I'd sort of splat up against the wall and then slither down it with no control over my body. Eddy and I both got our necks snapped. That hurts. That was a very confusing night. Like all of a sudden out of nowhere I was lying on my back in the weirdest position and Eddy was just kneeling over me with all this blonde hair in my face saying "Hi, there," and all I could think of was if Mom or Dad walked into the room and saw that, because all he was really doing was looking for a pillow. I think I passed out three times that night. . . .

Then there was only Rob, Laurel and me left in the car and we dropped Laurel off in Cambridge at Martha's house to spend the night. We refilled our squirt guns. . . . At 2:30 we went down to drive for the LRY [Liberal Religious Youth] paper drive. Rob and I were sitting in the front seats (squirting away) and Richard sat in the back telling us how rude it was. . . . He rolled down my seat so my head was in his lap, but then when he noticed how repulsed I was by this gross show of vulgarity, he finally put it back up. (I thought he only went for Laurel!!) . . .

After the drive . . . [we] read some underground comics and then we went out into the middle of the street loaded with warm water and soaked everybody. . . . It was cold out, but it was fun. . . .

I still can't get over what Frank and Susan did last Monday morning. Frank called around 9:00 and said he'd be over. He was there within a half hour. He picked her up and they went to "Lover's Lane." They went through the old parking routine, and, being very up-lifted, decided to have a little fun. There was this red car parking near-by, so Frank pulls up beside it. They sit for a while and then Sue gets out and offers them a cigarette. They didn't want any. The girl tried to pull on her clothes, but she got stuck under the steering wheel. Well, soon after, Frank and Susan decided that they were hungry. So they went down to "First National"'s and got some pop-corn and Coke. They went back to "Lover's Lane" where the red

car still was, and this time Frank parks nose to nose with
it. The "guys" are making it in the front seat, so Frank
and Sue sit on the hood of Frank's car eating pop-corn
and drinking soda: staring into their front seat. Like watching an x-rated movie free!! Crazy! I guess a feeling of
generosity found itself in Frank because after a while
longer Frank got up and offered them pop-corn. They
didn't want that either. Frank and Sue kept ambling over
and being neighborly and catching them in various stages
of undress. Like she'd be lying there with her skirt hoisted
above her waist fumbling with her underwear while he
was sitting there struggling with his pants. Poor things.
Well, Sue has to go to school at 12:20 'til 5:00 so eventually Frank had to pick up her books and drive her
there, which was too bad.

Reading these passages one might have said that Vivienne
showed a normal appetite for life. But after the first week in
April, there were signs in her journal of the return of her depression. John May had gone and she missed Jeff Lob and Mike
Nelson as well. She felt overwhelmed by homework and developed an undiagnosed abdominal illness accompanied by fever
that made her miss some school.

April 10, 1973
I have been out of school a lot lately. Three weeks ago,
I went to Maine with Laurel and Daddy and that meant
that I was absent all five days that week. Then last week
I was sick Wednesday and Thursday, and this week I was
absent today (maybe tomorrow too at this rate). What
happened to get me sick this week is this: Last night
(Monday night) Laurel and I went to Trinity to sing in
the Bach. About halfway through, I began to get these
terrible stabs of pain. I had been feeling really hot all

along, but when I first got that pain, the heat washed over me and stayed broiling the entire night. . . . We were going to leave after the first half. As it happened, so were Doug and Richard [friends of Laurel and Vivienne's]. Doug was going to give Richard a ride home, so we got a ride. At first I said that I would like to get a little air, so I asked Doug to let me off at the corner of Main and the Fellsway. Doug drove and Richard sat in the front seat with him (Doug has a VW bus) and Laurel and I sat in the back seat. Laurel was sitting [in] the normal and accepted way of sitting in a car and I was lounging with my feet up on the seat and my back against the wall of the bus, when this *really* awful stab of pain came and I thought I was going to die. But instead I bolted upright and then doubled over in the seat and more heat surged over me. At this point we were nearing the corner of Main and the Fells and Doug called back, "Do you want me to let you out up here?" I knew I couldn't walk so I called, "You'd better drive me all the way." He said, "You don't feel too well, do you?" and I said, "No." When I got in the door, I was really shaking and crying. Mommy wanted me rushed down to the hospital to see if I had appendicitis, but I've never wanted to go near a doctor who was going to explore those regions, ever since [I was] checked to find out if I was pregnant or not. I mean, I would have told him anyway. . . .

The fever and pain subsided and hospitalization proved unnecessary. But Vivienne continued to feel tired for several days.

Her reference to an examination "to explore those regions" has a history. When Vivienne was ten years old, she had an experience that colored her trust of doctors for the rest of her life. A physician was visiting another ill member of the family. "I forget who was sick," Paulette said later, "but he noticed that Vivienne looked a little bloated. She had this fat tummy.

She felt all her life that she was too fat. So he said, 'Bring her around to the office next week and we'll examine her,' so of course I took her. Well, he got her into that office by herself and put her onto the examining table, and without a word of explanation, he gave her a gynecological exam. It was brutal, completely unexpected. I had no idea..."

Even the good news that she had been awarded a scholarship to the Cambridge School of Weston, and would be going there next fall, failed to relieve Vivienne's recurrent and now alarming depression.

April 11, 1973

I am worthless. I am of no use to anyone, and no one is of any use to me. What good to kill myself? How can you kill nothing? A person who has committed suicide has had at least something to end. He must know joy to know misery. I have known nothing. Why live? Why die? One is an equal choice to the other. What do I do? I wonder if love would change anything. I don't know anymore. To know that the future looks worse doesn't help me any. I need people and there aren't any who care. It takes tolerance not to give in to death.

The same day she made this journal entry, Vivienne wrote a poem expanding on the last thought she had written in her journal.

la faim — hunger

It takes tolerance
Not to give in to death,
To resist the temptation
How easy just to die.
To keep on living an empty life
Takes patience from an empty person.

Tolerance . . . .

How long do you wait
When nothing has come?
It becomes harder to resist;
You waver by the edge of the sea.
It takes tolerance
Not to give in to death.

In May of that year, Vivienne was finishing her schoolwork at Cambridge Friends and looking forward to the family vacation in Maine. But her poetry reveals that the loss of John May still cut deeply and that she felt both imprisoned in her life and helpless.

May 14, 1973
WHERE IS NIGHT?

I notice that day is gone
And where is night?
You took the sun, but why
Can't you leave me the moon?
It's all right. I understand
That time is scarce
And days are few.
But you could have
Left me the night
So that I could remember you . . .
You took the sun, but why
Can't you leave me the moon?

May 14, 1973
GOOD BYE

It comes so slowly,
Like a tinnitus in your ear.

They'll think you're insane;
It's nothing they can hear.
But I know It's there;
You have so much to lose,
I'll keep your treasures
When It has taken you.

They'll imprison you
And try to take your mind.
But that is one thing
That they cannot do
Because you left it behind. And
All the world has seen you crash,
And I know that sound has ended.
But Hey,
That's no way
To say good bye.

On May 16 her poem expressed a sense of futility, and on May 17 she reflected on her helplessness.

1

You are fenced in
It's no use to try
To see through;
You can't even
See out.

Seeing is comprehending
And that you can never do
You need the finest of sight
And that you can never have
While you are here.

Time passes slowly
While you are sitting here

There is no escape!
No use climbing the steely fence;
The fence is higher
Than all your life stacked up
For you are a prisoner
Of your world.

2

Your day is full
Of Paris Peace Talks
Five alarm fires
And a protest grenade.

Nine to five
And back again
Traffic jams
And a luncheon delay

I ask you why
You do this
Day in and day out
And you reply:

"I can't ignore
The problems of this world
I cannot run away"
But I will say:

"My day is full
Of songs of soul
Cold clear water
Brimming smiles

Sun shining through
Tall trees in bloom
Limitless time
To live . . ."

You have taken time
Not to miss
The problems of the world
But you have forgotten
    The joyful tear beside you.
    (You have run away!)

Early in June, as school was ending, Vivienne wrote to John May of her increasing despair.

Thursday night
June 5, 1973

Dear Mr. May,

How are you doing? Do you know I still miss you? Even though you've been gone a very long time. I hope that you are happy. What is California like?

Will you please write, and send it Airmail? My last letter to you I didn't send Airmail because we didn't have enough stamps. But this time I'll try to. Otherwise, even if you answered promptly (which is a fantasy I don't even indulge in dreaming up!), there would be approximately a month's interval of time before I received anything back from you. You don't know what joy it would afford me if you would answer my letters! (No matter how long it takes!) But really, please do! Enough of that!

How did you fare driving across the country? Did you run into too much gas rationing? (That's good ole "Tricky Dick" managing the state of affairs in all his usual splendor!) Did you drive the whole distance by yourself? It must have been beautiful to get there in the end, anyway.

And now I must say something and it's not easy. You see there have been a lot of tears lately. Not where anyone would see, but just by myself. I think I'm lonely or something related to it. But there's nobody about who can help me. I was just wondering if you would please send me something encouraging, positive, anything! for me to live on for a while. It's funny, but I've really gone to pieces. I remember my mother saying how you commented on how nice and good our family is. But sometimes the family can't help. Not with this. I've lost faith in everything. It sounds so dramatic, and yet it's true. I am asking you as a friend to help me. I would be so grateful. Yours,

Vivienne

P.S. This is really one of the strangest letters that I've ever written anybody. I wonder if I'll ever actually send it to you.
P.S.S. Please don't be upset with me if you do get it. It's a terrible letter, I know.

Soon after this John came east for two months on his way to Europe and went to Vivienne's graduation as he had promised he would. He found her sullen and distant and they spent little time together. He telephoned but she was not at home. She was cheered, perhaps by John May's brief return, or by a short family trip to Maine.

Tuesday night, 10:00 P.M.
June 26, 1973

Dear John, alias "beautchus,"

I am very sorry that I missed your call. However, I hear that you had a merry chat with "My Little Princess." Isn't she cute? ("My Little Princess" is a name which I have recently taken to calling Mummy. She always replies, "You mean 'The Old Hag Witch'?" She's silly!) I really would have liked to say a last goodbye to you before you finally left. . . .

"My Little Princess" has finished the Oriental rug that she was working on. Betsy [the family dog] loves to sleep on it. It's just her size, you see.

It's Mommy's birthday and anniversary on Thursday the 28th, and Daddy, Laurel and I (while up in Maine) stopped at a Scandanavian Imports shop and I got Mommy a medium-blue and white enameled bowl. . . . It seems I am the only person with any money around here. And I want you to know that I have earned it all myself! . . .

I guess that you've heard that we're *moving*. The negative financial ramifications of that are that Mommy will have to commute and Laurel and I will have to five-day board. But we always have pulled through, and we will again. It must seem morbid to think about money so much, but money is one of those things where the less there is, the more you think about it. But of course I am very excited about moving! The prospect keeps me going. "My Princess" is much brighter and shines more now, although the actual process of moving will doubtless take *a lot* out of her. But she is brave and has already started packing up clothes, dishes, etc. We should be moving in sometime in early October. I wish you could see the house! It has two front stairways and one back stairway (. . . forgot to tell you that it is in the middle of Gloucester on a street parallel to Main). We have named some of the rooms. Dad's study downstairs is to be called "Toad Hall" (from "Wind in the Willows"), which is not a bad resemblance. The music room next to that doesn't have a name yet. Also downstairs is a spacious kitchen, a dining room and my parents' living room. Upstairs we each have our own rooms, which are not yet named except for Mommy and Daddy's which is to be called "Lovers' Leap" with the subtitle of "Paulette's Web." On the other side of the wall from that is the kids' living room which is to be called "The Diogenese Club" (from a Sherlock Holmes novel). Next or near to that room is a bathroom which is now named "The Watergate." There are several small spare rooms at the back of the house which will be put to different uses, two attic rooms, and a cellar which can be used only for heating the house (half gas — half coal!).

Laurel wants to put a Japanese garden at one end of the back yard, Rob and I want to leave part of the yard wild, and Mommy wants to fill the entire place with a massive flower garden. It should prove an interesting yard.

The move is hardest for Daddy. He always finds decisions, transitions, and transactions hard to make. But he'll come through. He knows we're all here to help him.

Maine was beautiful, and I thought of you every time I looked at Pumpkin Island (which wasn't very often because there was a pea soup fog blanketing the place almost the entire time). I always feel better once I've been in Maine. No matter what the weather. It always brings you up again.

I've got to stop writing about things over here now, because just as soon as I think of one thing, I've thought of two others, and I'm afraid I've probably already severely strained your eyes.

You told my mother that you would *really* try and write, and I hold you to that. I want to know how you're doing and what you will be doing. Have you gained thousands of pounds now that you're staying with your parents? Will you be teaching any English at all? (You should be!!) Do you still have your dog Froida (is that right?)? Write me a nice, big, long letter — or better yet, make it hundreds of short (or long!) ones! All the more mail for me!

It's past 12:00 P.M. now and I'm the only one up so I'll

have to lock up the house soon. I'll send you our new address when I find out what it is! Be sure and do the same for me when you change your address. I'll keep writing you until you feel compelled out of sheer embarrassment (sp?) to write me back! I hope that you're enjoying your summer (tell me about your spring travels!!).

I trust that you realize that we all miss you very much here and would be extremely happy to hear from you. Much love from all of us,

Vivienne

P.S. Do you think that the American public will listen to Dean or Nixon?
[turtle drawing] ... The Tender Tardy Turtle

Despite the more cheerful tone of the letter it was at about this time that Vivienne first shared her suicidal thoughts with Laurel, and death itself began to take on for her a concrete and compelling quality. In her journal she described her first attempt to strangle herself.

This is the night of July 9; a Monday. I have spent the past half hour in the back bathroom trying to strangle myself, and sending a prayer. The prayer was not strong enough. I never could pray. You can tell when a prayer doesn't get through. I believe it is a sign to check with the validity and sincerity of it.

But I have been able to practice how to strangle [myself] all the same. I know that I will need the knowledge some day soon. There are two effects to clutching your throat. I have not had enough time to study the reasons for this. However, one is life and one is death. Life comes in the form of a whitened face and a sensation of tingling through your whole body while you sway back and forth. When you let go, you make jerking motions with increasing speed. This is the more horrifying of the two effects. Death comes as an increasingly darkening face and unstrained thin breathing, which I am sure would soon die away altogether. Your head pounds painfully and in the mirror I had the privilege to see for myself what my dead face will look like immediately after the killing. Somehow this effect is much less upsetting than the first. Perhaps this is a sign that my prayers are being considered.

With regard to my family: I realize that my death will upset their lives; some more than others. However, I am sure now that I would upset their lives more by staying on here and living this life. Surely they do not deserve it. They will never realize what I have spared them. I will go with the knowledge. I hope it is a kindness to everybody. I have loved them very much.

DEATH IS GOING TO BE A BEAUTIFUL THING she wrote across the downstairs bathroom wall.

On the back of this journal entry, she wrote the following poem:

> *You are watching it drift,*
> *That elusive peaceful dream.*
> *In the tumult and confusion*
> *It becomes salient and hypnotic*
> *The echoing tinnitus conveys certain doom.*
>
> *The dream is drawn and closed;*
> *The dark is somehow frightening.*
> *Silence shatters the quiet*
> *In quick and sudden frenzy:*
> *They'll never know you're gone.*

The next day she wrote again to John May. She reported her suicide attempt in detail. She may have felt relieved temporarily by her strangling experiment because she spoke of her determination to live for another year. In the four poems she included there are references to death.

July 10, 1973
Tuesday, 9:40 P.M.

Dear Mr. May,

Would you *please* write? You know it's very hard to write to a person when you don't even know where he's at! How about a letter? Do I hear a post card? Anything!

Now you get to find out where I'm at! (Lucky you!) There's some good news and some bad news. First the bad news: I've just gone through a spell of finally giving up. I actually calculated the best way to die, and decided on and practised strangling myself. I told myself that I was not being selfish towards my family because they would be better off watching me die than watching me live this life. That's actually probably true, but I've decided to torture them and give it another year. I was really serious, but again I have decided to stick this life of mine out — for the time being at least. (I'm glad I didn't go into any of the details.)

The good news is, that through all of this, today I suddenly started to write again! I'm so happy! I can't tell you! But I thought I might send you what I wrote today. Would you read them, and if you have the time, please criticize me on them? That would be a great help. Tell me if you find any clichés or anything like that, especially! I wrote these poems under the influence of Joni Mitchell's "For the Roses." Does it show? Let me know if there is one you particularly like or dislike. I'll be interested. Well, I'll start writing them on the back of this page. This one is particularly about my day today:

EMPTY SUNSHINE DAY
Silence in your ears
The riots in your tears —

Just an empty
Sunshine Day.
Sit in the sun
... no alternatives
Required
Of your life.
Time on your hands,
Life on your mind;
Did you ever
Really understand?
Who knows
Your martyred life
Just a bitter dream,
An endless comma,
Just an empty
Sunshine Day.

JOYS OF LIVING

The Stock Exchange,
Neon signs,
Traffic jams,
Indo China,
Another exam and the Watergate.
New train tables,
Inflation, highway repairs,
Nixon,
His dog "Checkers,"
Your new bugged home ...
It's all too late!

DEPARTURE

This is written about that whole death
syndrome I just went through:

Seagulls squawk
  The sun goes down
  Tarnished in the dusk
  Sinking low to a tune
  You made up for love . . .
  But it's something
  Crazy you're hearing!
  Not an empty voice
  From the hollows
  Of your heart . . .
  A loud resounding crash
  In the black
  And shiny night.
The moon glazes over
  The inky murk
  Of the sea.
  Seagulls leave you
  In your surprise.
  Stars laugh in your face,
  The moon weeps in your eyes
  . . . Leave the cruel night . . .
  Plunge deep in the tidal waters
  . . . Cold dash of sorrow . . .
  Bitter-sweet breezes
  Sweep the last of your dreams
  Away with you.

DREAM OF REALITY
  Deep blue steel
  Lions mane
  You do a
  Pole vault
  Into your dreams.

But why do you land
Crushed by the song
Of a nightingale
On the wing?

Or study the distorted
Lines of wisdom
On the face of the old man
Lying quietly in the shade?

The nightingale
In the branches above
In consistence there
With the still of her companion.

What is it?
The stillness of wisdom?
The patience of doom?
That drives you to mount
That coal-black stallion?

Why is it
That you suddenly know
With certainty
That you cannot stay astride?

He throws you
In your madness!...
You are alone again;
Away from the truthful dreams
That frighten you so ...

... I have nothing else to write so I won't. I'll just say
that I hope you'll write me, so I'll know how you are.
And smile.

With love,

Vivienne

Two days later Vivienne wrote John again. The letter is matter-of-fact in tone and describes activities with friends. A sentence near the end, therefore, comes as something of a surprise: "I wish so much I had some friends to be with but I don't, so I'm writing this one." That same day she wrote a poem, "Empty Sparrow," that captured her dark mood:

July 12, 1973

EMPTY SPARROW

I heard it in the trees
Last night
Away up there.
Something lost
And never found;
A song of joy,
Yet somehow
Mimed and mute.

Wistful leaves
And whimsical trees,
And empty pounding
In the heart
Of an old and weary
Sparrow:
Heavy
On black and white night.

Enraged and excited
Ravens
Swoop to devour
A deathly still sparrow
Lying so quietly there
In scattered leaves
Just below
A dazed and silent tree.

I heard it in the trees
Last night
Away up there.
Something lost
And never found;
A song of joy,
Yet somehow
Mimed and mute.

Six days later she wrote a letter to John that she never sent. Her father's future in Gloucester, which clearly troubled her, was not quite decided. Vivienne complained that her depression was interfering with her poetry writing.

July 18, 1973
10:30 P.M.

Look what I just found! The two letters (to my about ten) you ever wrote me! Must be lonely for them, a mere *two* (ahem!) — Anyway, they're very interesting! The first one is dated 6/22/71 and is all about writing poems. It has made me realize two things. First, that I've lost some of the sparkle and brilliance I once felt for poetry, but second, you pointed out that language is a poet's tool and that a poet can do what he wants with it. It is good for me to think of that now, because I seem to be in a rut as far as writing poems; they all sound exactly the same to me. So if I remember that, perhaps it will help.... I must be getting tired.

...I've gone on another diet and am actually losing weight! There is absolutely no willpower involved (obviously — I'm getting results)! It's my luck that nutrition is the *in* thing; now I can sit there, be cool and diet all at the same time! I've got it made. This weekend Dad has his campaign service in Gloucester — soon after, we should

get the word. I hope he lets them see what a truly wonderful person he really is! But I don't want to write any
more about this — I get nervous just thinking about it!

John was living with a friend in San Francisco at the time
and there were delays in his receiving correspondence. He wrote
on July 17 and Vivienne received the letter on the twenty-first.
He apologized for the delay and told her that, for an unknown
reason, it was difficult for him to write letters. His letter was
— as always when he did write — caring, supportive and full
of news. He would be starting a job in September, teaching
English to high-school freshmen.

He tried to address her depression but could not be aware
of its depths.

You know, I've now taught many students. With many
of them I'm able to establish a sense of friendship. But
there are some whom I treasure because I gain so much
just from knowing them. You are one of those people. I
fear that any praising I do of you, you don't believe, but
I'm going to say it anyway. You, Vivienne Loomis, are a
unique and special person with a beauty that stems from
the center and reaches out. You have a quick mind, physical beauty, compassion, gentleness and honesty which add
much to my life and to the lives of those around you.

It has been a tough time for you lately, so your letters
say. That's OK, tough times come. You said that you had
spent a great deal of time crying lately, and that's the best
way to handle feeling low. But, it works much better if
you can cry with somebody there who you know loves
you so that you can have [that person] to make sure you
know it's OK to be sad but that you'll move through it
to feeling glad again. The person who is with you should
just let you cry without telling you answers. The best

ones are the ones you find for yourself. Maybe you and
Laurel could work out a deal where you could say "Hey
Laurel — I need to cry, could you just listen to me and be
with me for a while." And then when she needs it you
could do the same for her.

Please feel free to write me in whatever mood you're in.

Vivienne wrote again the day she received John's letter.

July 21, 1973
Saturday noon (approximately)
Dear Mr. May, John May, John,

...Dad preaches [in Gloucester] tomorrow. Then later
they have a parish meeting and vote on whether to invite
him or not. I get nervous just thinking about it.

You know, I wish that Laurel and I could help each
other the way you suggest, but Laurel has gone on an
independence binge, and is not very accessible. Especially since she made the acquaintance of some gentlemen
friends.... Laurel spends a large part of the day and most
of the night [with them].... She is very close friends
with [one of them] and fairly good friends with the others.
She and [one of them] are too close, which has caused
Laurel some problems of her own. Plus — she's always
good and stoned whenever she comes back from over
there, so she's never in the mood to talk at all, let alone
anything serious. I suppose I would listen to her if she
needed it, but she doesn't want it. I mean, she makes it
sound as though it's a privilege for me to know what she's
doing! Don't get me wrong! We are still very close, but
we're both just a bit touchy now, and don't do very well
together. Perhaps the self-centeredness of both of us is
showing up at the same time right now.

Actually, I like most of the people ... though I disapprove of what Laurel does.... But you can't rule someone else's life, can you? You see, Laurel and I have got the same basic problem. We both are very lonely and seek human ties. However, she seems to be satisfied with the physical aspect, whereas I crave a more spiritual relationship where physical love is an outlet of something much deeper and more personal than mere physical pleasure. It's obvious to me now that one is a lot harder to come by than the other. I can see now that I won't be sending you this letter; it's too much like a soap opera. I'll sign off now, before I waste any more paper. I'll try to write you a real letter tomorrow.

> With love,
>
> *Vivienne*

The family went to Maine for their summer vacation on August 1. A week later Vivienne wrote John a long letter discussing her struggle with moral values. The letter was begun on August 8 and started with chatty news of Laurel and a summer friend. She continued in earnest the next afternoon:

> ... Tonight is another square dance. Last week I didn't dance even one dance because nobody knew me and I wasn't in the mood to ask anybody; I usually do. What a bore that was! Tonight will probably be different because Laurel, [a girl friend] and I have gotten to know several ... [camp] counselors ... and though these dudes probably won't dance, they come and sit around in their van and we can talk to them, etc. The only trouble with these counselors is that they never do anything as a group; all but three will leave, if we're all sitting together, and then those three pair off with we three. I find this more or less amusing. The method is to the effect of "Hi. I'm Dick.

Let's go for a long walk." Sometimes I laugh in their face. Of course, that reaction does get me a lot of friends. To tell the truth, though, these fellows are most of them basically morons anyway, so it doesn't bother me. Laurel has become friends with a fairly decent chap . . . and [her girl friend] with a little less desirable fellow. . . . I myself have managed to stay unattached, thanks to my unfailing lack of charm. Only one guy tried to rape me five days ago, and I haven't seen him since. Mommy and Daddy would have a fit if they knew, but I didn't find it as traumatic as everybody seems to make it. The fact is that this particular fellow had already had a few six packs too many. It had nothing to do with me. Well, so much for the "Dirt of the Day." That's about all the excitement that there has been recently. Tonight is the square dance, tomorrow night is the dress rehearsal for the . . . show over at [the camp], and then we'll probably go again to the production itself the following night. Mommy and Daddy are leaving for Monhegan Island on Saturday morning, and will stay there about five days. I'm not sure what their plans are after that.

And now I don't know where to start or whether I should talk with (write to) anybody about it, but I'm going to because it's what's heaviest on my mind, and you're the only one ever even vaguely understood my mind. I'd talk to my parents, but it would depress them too much; I'm their youngest daughter. For you I'm another student who likes and trusts you. My parents have an unbelievable amount of problems of their own. If this gets too personal or uncomfortable for you, I'm sorry and I apologize. Please just let me know if you'd rather not talk about these things.

I don't know where to start. I wish you were here to talk to. . . . Do you remember last summer when you were up here? One of the things that you told me then was that I expected sometimes too much of myself. You'd be so disappointed in me now. It's almost as if I didn't expect anything of myself anymore. For instance, the fact that I smoke. I used to tell myself that it was just a sign of weakness and that I would always be able to stand on my own two feet. For a year I was very cool and whenever the pipe was passed to me I just said "Thanks, but no thanks." But this year Rob was home, as selfish and blind as ever. And I'm not just insulting him; he really, honestly is. That is hard enough to live with, but what it did to the family and Mommy in particular is too much. Mommy would come home from work exhausted. Rob whittled her down to nothing and I almost went crazy trying to live with the two of them. Mommy came to me for help. And I really have helped her whenever I could. But it puts a certain pressure on me; I'm not even fourteen yet, and Mommy's forty-eight. All the pressure and tension mounted up and I snapped. I decided that I couldn't be as perfect as wanted and I had to have some outlet. I've been smoking grass since around January. I've gotten stoned often enough, but I never really enjoyed it. Usually I just get high enough to relax. I can't seem to do that normally anymore. Mommy knows because I told her, and she understands but disapproves. Daddy knows too, and I guess he feels the same way. The family situation has affected Daddy in a similar way; he drinks more than he used to. He couldn't take things any more than Mommy could and he finally took counseling this spring. I don't know how much it has helped him. I think that it has pointed out a lot of problems that he's just not ready to cope with yet. I suppose *Laurel* has had some of the hardest problems this year. She has known [this one boy] for over two years now and has been seriously in love with him for one year. I have never disapproved of the fact that they had sex together, because I consider it natural when you *love* somebody. And they always took every precaution. But they have agreed not to be committed to each other; [he] lives ... [out of state] and cannot always be there. At any rate Laurel is not very discriminating. ... The fact is that she really needs constant love, and this creates both physical and mental problems for her. She has known all along that I disapproved of fucking anyone but the one you love. I still feel that, and that's why I wouldn't fuck [a boy] five nights ago. It's as simple as that. But you suddenly realize how very hard it is to have so many morals in today's world. It seems like nobody else believes in sex *because* of love. They all seem to take it more as just sex per se. I just can't see that! Sometimes I wonder if I'm *really* right or not. And sometimes I wonder if the advice that I give Mommy is the best. I'm only (not even quite!) fourteen! But as far as smoking grass is concerned, I've just decided that I'm only human and I can only carry so much alone with no help. I would rather that it were another human being that were helping me, not to relax, but to solve these problems. However, there is nobody. The family helps each other, but you really need outside contact almost more right now.

I'm almost sorry to have burdened you with all of this, and I'll stop now. It's just that it was so much on my mind that I couldn't write you without talking about it. I hope that you don't mind too much.

I wish you were here. Say hello to Fran for me and write soon.

With love,

Vivienne

The Little Brown Jug was not the haven it had been other summers. Each member of the family was under strain. The counseling that Vivienne mentions was actually a series of vocational and psychological tests David had undergone, the beginning of his investigation to determine whether or not he should remain in the ministry. Laurel was a restless sixteen and felt somewhat impatient with Vivienne's monitoring and moral scruples.

The neighboring camp was a center of activity. This made the summer eventful for Laurel, but for Vivienne it was an intrusion. She felt uneasy around the young men who came to socialize with her sister.

"Vivienne sometimes got plagued by the counselors," Laurel said. "Like two guys would come up to us and really start coming on strong. She'd start kissing me and say, 'Well, I'm already taken.' Sometimes she just told them to drop dead. She had another trick. She would pretend to faint. Her eyes would actually roll back. She would just go limp as if she had dropped dead. She did this a couple of times. I remember one night one of the boys ran to me and said, 'Something's wrong with your sister.' It really freaked him out. Her breathing became shallow as if she were in a coma. Then I'd put her to bed and the boys would leave. It was fun. We used to laugh about it."

While Paulette and David were in the household, Vivienne felt some protection. This particular summer, David and Paulette had been invited to take a five-day vacation with friends on Monhegan Island. They were due to leave August 11. Paulette felt that she could leave the girls for this short time since there were close neighbors. The trip happened to include August 14, Vivienne's fourteenth birthday, but Paulette planned to celebrate it at another time. As it turned out, the friends were unable to go and David and Paulette set out alone for the island, some eight hours away. Vivienne was left alone in the house with Laurel.

Four poems Vivienne wrote on August 15 and 16 reflect her mood. Her metaphors suggest fear of her own desires and of abandonment:

Pretty sparrow
Sit still
While the winds
They are callin'
Never leave them
At dawn
Till the ravens
Have gone

The earth stands still
In your cold
Dark morning
Crystalizing
Your fears
Tied in knots
'Round your throat
Pretty sparrow

Pretty sparrow
Love your skies
When freedom
Crashes down
Love your shelter
Oldest trees
While the winds
They are callin'

Revelation
Of dawn
Cast off flight
Soft breezes
Calling you
And mute birds
Shall sing
My pretty sparrow.

Two painters talk
Of bitter and love
And capture it there
In canvas and oil.
Powerful hands
That brush together
Lines that make you
Dimly remember
Life's loving and kind.

The people shuffle
Softly from corner to corner
Quite suddenly snared
By that picture
Hanging there.
That small dab of grey
Has definitely made
That fantastic splash of yellow
Into a setting sun.

Wednesday, August 15, 1973, 8:15 P.M.

The next day Vivienne wrote two other troubled poems:

Now is the time
You wait so long
Rationalize
Your thoughts
"Perfect Soul"

Stay quiet
From day to day
Keep your imperfections
On a close rein.
They'll never guess.

So easy now
Quite free
Just once don't
Be unselfish
They'll think you're mad.

Now is the time
You've waited so long
Rationalizing
But deeper still
You're no "Perfect Soul."

PROUD-HEADED
QUEEN OF THOUGHTS
    Dance
    To the fire
    Proud-headed
    Queen
    Of thoughts.

    Outdance
    The flames
    Craze the sparks
    That dare fly
    Your way.

    Nothing left
    Nobody there
    So dance
    And sing
    In the fire.

    So many
    Intricate steps
    Composed
    By you in this
    Calculated mistake.

Dance on!!

Dance
To the fire
Proud-headed
Queen
Of thoughts.

August 16, the day of her parents' return, began badly. Vivienne and Laurel had an argument. Laurel thought she might be pregnant and Vivienne was upset. She was angry at Laurel for not taking the situation more seriously.

"I wasn't that concerned," Laurel said. "I always knew my parents would help if I needed it. I guess I sort of denied the problem too." Vivienne was furious at Laurel's casual attitude.

By evening Vivienne felt very depressed and angry. Laurel had a date with one of the counselors. She was planning to go out to dinner and be away for the evening.

Vivienne and Laurel had two long-term summer friends in the Maine community. Vivienne was particularly close to one of them and when she began to date the camp counselors, along with Laurel, Vivienne felt especially left out. Both friends were there that night.

"I just had this date," Laurel said. "I was getting dressed to go out. Vivienne had been moody all day. I think she felt deserted. She gave me all these nutty reasons about why I shouldn't go out." Laurel continued to prepare for her evening. Vivienne alternated between silence and argument.

"Finally she got very mad at me because I wouldn't change my plans," Laurel said. "The next thing I knew, a half hour before I was supposed to go out, she said, 'If you go out, I'm going to take these pills.' There were some prescription cold pills in the bathroom. I said, 'Listen, I want to go out. Are you going to do it?' and she said, 'Yes.' She ran to the bathroom and started swallowing these pills." Laurel was uncertain about how seriously she should take this gesture. She felt exasperated with her sister. "I thought to myself, 'OK, we'll see how far this has to go.'" Then Vivienne "was just going about her business, walking around getting a glass of water, and going into her room and disappearing, lying down. She looked perfectly normal. I was supposed to go to this dinner dance and she wasn't invited. Now she was trying to make me stay home. I watched her. Every once in a while, she'd drop her head in her hands.

"I didn't know what to do," Laurel said. "She wouldn't talk to me. She went into her room and told me to leave her alone." Laurel talked with their friends about what should be done. She was dressed to go and her date had already come. Finally, when she realized that Vivienne had taken all the pills, she called her parents.

Paulette remembers that "Laurel called up absolutely hysterical. She said, 'Vivienne is taking pills.' David asked to speak with her on the telephone and she refused to talk to him. I said, 'If she looks the least bit hazy-eyed get her to Blue Hill Hospital, get her stomach pumped, get help immediately. We'll be right up.'"

"I was really angry," Laurel said. "By this time Vivienne was sitting in the living room. The guy I was with said to Vivienne, 'When you die, will you give me your flute?' That made me furious at him. Vivienne hardly spoke to any of us. I told [my girl friend] to go get her mother. This made Vivienne mad. I kept checking Vivienne. She seemed hostile but she didn't seem that sick."

At about two in the morning Paulette and David, and Rob as well, arrived at the Little Brown Jug. "We were all frantic, but I guess by that time Vivienne was sorry she refused to talk to us on the phone. She walked out of the house and gave David a big hug. When we sat down and talked, Vivienne told us about Laurel's possible pregnancy."

The family talked long into the early morning hours. The

concern quickly switched from Vivienne to Laurel, who had not had a period for two or three months. Paulette was anxious to have Laurel checked medically. "The attention got diverted to me," Laurel said. "As far as I remember most of the conversation was about finding a doctor and a hospital to have me examined. I think my parents felt that they had left Vivienne too near her birthday and without enough security. I think they thought she was angry with me and that the issue would get resolved. Mostly, that night, they reassured her. I don't think the pills did any real damage. It was serious to them, but not as serious as my problem."

On August 21 Vivienne received a long letter from John May that he had begun on July 31 and taken up again on August 19. He provided news of his own moves, told of nervousness about starting teaching again, offered warm reassurance, took a moderate position on marijuana smoking, and said that he agreed in principle with her attitudes about sex, but suggested that she was a bit inflexible. He provided a more liberal view she was not able to use. "The 'morality' of the nation has changed," he wrote. "I used to think that sex was to be saved for marriage, now I'm sure it's connected with some type of love feeling for someone."

The next day Vivienne wrote to John describing the whole incident.

8:00 P.M. Wednesday night
August 22, 1973

Dear Mr. May,

I'm sorry for this first part of this letter. But I just have to tell you about it so that you can understand what I'm thinking about.

Last Thursday night I sort of snapped. I mean, I became disgusted with *everything,* and for the first time in a really long time I got a really selfish streak. In the after-

noon Laurel and I had a terrible fight. Her friend [s ———
and ———] ... were here, but I didn't care. It was all
about how my problems couldn't be Laurel's, as she had to
have her own life, but I said that I needed her right now,
and couldn't she help me? She said that [a boy] ... needed
her too. I said who was more important? I was irrational
and so was she. In the end, I said "OK, have another evening with [your boyfriend]. You *may* see me whenever
you get in." (She was eating out with [the boy] and then
spending the evening with him where he was staying.)
Then I walked into the bathroom, spotted some cold pills
(prescription) which were fairly powerful, and swallowed
about four. Then I took the bottle with the remaining
pills (about twelve left) and shut the door behind me in
my room. Laurel stood outside justifying herself to [her
girl friends] and nobody was paying the slightest attention
to me, so I took a few more pills. I sat there and told
myself that I just couldn't handle all of Mummy's problems (which she invariably brings to me now), Daddy's
problems, Laurel's problems, and most of all my problems.
I said, damn the family. I've carried them long enough,
now I'll do something for myself. Then I walked out of
the room and went to the bathroom. I could feel a chill
and a fever coming on. After I went to the bathroom (to
kill myself not just to go to the room) I stayed in the
living room and picked up a magazine to read while waiting for [this boy] to come and pick Laurel up. Everybody was going around whispering to each other and
Laurel was getting dressed to go out. Finally [he] came,
and *they* whispered together, and then Laurel came in
and said, "Vivienne, are you going to kill yourself or not?
I mean, I'm not going to go to any trouble if you're not."
I said, "Oh, no. You two run along. Have a nice night."
She said, "What are you going to do? I mean, I could get

in a lot of trouble. You're my responsibility!" (Mummy and Daddy were away.) I said sarcastically, "Oh well! That changes the whole thing. Of course I wouldn't kill myself if it would hurt you!" "I'm going to call Mummy and Daddy." "Fine. You call tonight. I'll have to wait a day, a week, maybe even a month. When I *could* do it tonight. You know, it's merely a matter of inconvenience. You do what you want." She called. They talked and I forced myself to look at the newspaper in front of me. It was opened to ENGINEERING. "Daddy wants to talk to you, Vivienne. Please!" I had decided to leave all of this. I said "No." They talked longer and I forced myself to take in the words on the page. "Daddy wants to talk to you, Vivienne — he loves you!" I kept my eyes on the page. "No." "She's too damn proud," said [Laurel's date]. He was annoyed; I'd ruined his evening. Mummy and Daddy said not for Laurel to move — they'd be up as soon as possible with Rob, about 2:00 A.M. . . . Then [Laurel's boyfriend] drove back to [where] he was staying . . . and he smashed up (dented) [the] car hurrying over here.

I was back in my room when he got back with the car; he was mad as hell with me. I didn't care, I just reassured myself that this was the end. He said, "Proud of yourself, aren't you?" (about the car). By this time the few pills that I had taken were going into effect: I wasn't sick to my stomach at all, but my head was throbbing very hard, I had a terribly high fever, and every time I moved, my vision splintered up for a second. A few minutes later there was a slight tap on the door and [one of the girls] came in and sat down on the bed. She started to say something and started choking up. I rolled over and turned my back on her. Then she started reasoning with me. "If you just talk to me, maybe I can understand and help you." But the whole thing was that I didn't *want* her to understand. I wanted her to leave me alone and then maybe I could find some more pills or some rope — I could always suffocate myself if worst came to worst. I mean, I was all psyched up for "The End." It had to come! But after a while I realized that it wasn't going to come. The whole family would be up here and right now I was being watched like a hawk. So I cried a few minutes with Laurel, resigned myself to life again, and went out into the living room and laughed and talked with everybody. At 10:30 [Laurel's date] left. I kissed him goodbye and thanked him for everything. He said he was sorry about earlier in the evening (being mad). Everything was OK. At 2:00 A.M. the rest of the family arrived and I went outside and gave Daddy a big bearhug — I knew how much I had hurt him over the phone. Over the next day or so I talked with various people in my family, and they seemed to understand. Mummy said, "I don't see how anyone could stay sane with everyone pouring out all their problems to you — and you have no outlet..." But now she still brings me all her problems and loads me down, and I try to help her. Things are exactly the same as they were before... but maybe next time it gets like this, I'll have the strength to get up and start a new way of life; this time I was too worn out and tired.

This is all a very poor way of communicating this whole thing — I hope I got across what I wanted to. It's hard to really talk about this — it's not like most things I do in life that are all thought out beforehand and reasoned out in my mind. None of this was. I regret the whole thing. Not the way you regret something that's wrong, but because it was a waste of everyone's emotions and time and energy.

Oh God! If I could have gotten your letter a week ago!

You have no idea how much it did for me today! I miss
you so much sometimes. Just now I needed your clear
mind and the gifts you give from it. And you're right
about grass; you pointed out one thing to me which I
failed to notice before. And that is, that it is a lot *easier*
for me to show love (*not sex* — love) for people when
I'm high. But why should this be so? I can work on this.
It's healthy. Your letter has swung my mind around to
the positive side of things: Mummy has me go on walks
and sails and weaving, etc. which all leave me too much
time to reflect. It seems the more I reflect, the more dulled
my reflections become. So I welcomed your letter for
something fresh and clear. And it was! I apologize in a
way for all these letters. Just about every one is an appeal for help. Like a counseling service by mail! You must
get tired, no matter what you say in your letters; any
human being would. Would it help at all to know that
I love you, as a person? That I will try to help *you* any
time that *you* need it? I will, *any* time that I can!

This afternoon I wrote two poems (enclosed). I don't
know how good they are — perhaps you won't particularly like them at all, maybe you will. Tell me what you
think of them . . .

The letter ends with her response to his news.

One of the two poems she enclosed was a scornful description of "business men sitting around at big executive luncheons."
The other pictured another kind of inhumanity, indifference
to the pain of children.

> 5:00 Wednesday afternoon
> August 22, 1973
> *The chatter of children*
> *Who intrude on the noonday sun*
> *(And imposed on that)*

The impatient honk or curse
Of the executive
Coming home for lunch.

The neighborhood gossips
Only half notice at a sidelong glance
The rainbow smile, through tears
Amidst the everyday ordinary blanks
... As the peacock spreads his fan
(The ostrich's head in the sand)

Two neighborhood Housewives
Discussing that man across the street
(The town drunk)
With a half full bottle in one hand
And the other one holding up
A face of deserted smiles:

Whose crazy ups go down
And dreamed up dreams
Are not so unlike
The dreams of small children
Who play in the sun
And run and talk to you.

Of course, the neighborhood
Only half notices at a sidelong glance
The rainbow smile, oblivion
Amidst the everyday ordinary blanks
... As the peacock spreads his fan
(The ostrich's head in the sand.)

The summer was ending. But Paulette believed that in the days left Vivienne could improve if she were kept busy. "I tried to give her a larger picture," Paulette said later. "Maybe that wasn't right. Maybe it was erroneous, but at the same time I made her a program of sailing and handicrafts. Think about other people. Think about the world, I told her. I thought that would restore her perspective. I remember telling her to write John May too. I thought it would help her. I thought the problem would pass." But, as Vivienne wrote John, her mother's suggested walks and sailing and weaving "leave me too much time to reflect." Although Vivienne's crisis seemed to have been precipitated by Laurel's activities, her mother felt they were not connected. Paulette remarked later, "Laurel was only something to blame. I think the real trouble was that she couldn't deal with her depression. It was too painful and she hadn't lived long enough to know that one can weather pain. I think that's why she took the pills."

Vivienne wrote a poem that revealed her inner feeling of emptiness:

> *Is there no mirror?*
> *Nothing to echo back?*
> *I cannot find you!*
> *I have given all I have!*
> *Gotten nothing back.*
>
> *Are you so blind?!*
> *You cannot see*
> *You were given*
> *All I had.*
> *Now my arms*
> *Are empty.*

On August 23 Vivienne wrote her second letter in two days. She held her ground against John's more permissive sexual codes and repeated her wish to find sex linked with love.

11:00 A.M. Thursday
August 23, 1973

Dear Mr. May,

Surprise! Another letter from me. I'm talking about different things in this letter.

First, about your letter which was about *my* letter: You said that your morals on sex had changed both as you have grown and with the nation's. Maybe as I grow, things will change for me, but I don't think that I can follow the nation's trend; now the average girl puts down the last good book in the house and says, "Shit. Nothing else to do. I guess I'll go over to the stone wall on the corner and get picked up." I don't know. Three times, three people in the last 2½ weeks, have tried to fuck me. Twice I was good and stoned and once I was bored stiff. But each time, I just thought to myself — God! Is this all there is? Not only is there no true love, no giving — but this is all as routine as taking your vitamins in the morning. I don't see how you get Saturday night "fun" out of it. So I'll probably keep my ideals for the time being. Of course, I don't have, and never have had, any hang-ups about marriage. I just require a deep and caring love.

She wrote that she had decided that "grass" was not important in her life, and then offered *him* support in his anxiety about teaching.

I can see why you might be nervous about *five* freshmen classes (it'll be a definite change from Friends)! But I'm sure that you will come through with flying colors. There's just no way they couldn't like you, and just no way you couldn't make them learn if you wanted to. You're a fantastic teacher (even if I still can't spell, or write a grammatically correct sentence!). I remember when we were applying to CFS, Mrs. Stokes was talking to my parents, and she said, "You're very lucky to have Vivienne coming into the sixth grade. John May is really one of the best teachers we've ever had here." That's true, you can ask my mother! Really, *I* don't think you have anything to worry about!! (Chalk up another vote of confidence from across the country!)

Rob is off to Hampshire College (in Amherst) in the first week of September, Laurel and I start at Weston on September 10th. Mummy goes back to work the night of the day that Rob goes off to college (she's taking the *day* off to help him move in). We don't know when Daddy will start preaching down in Gloucester, we won't be actually moving *in* until early *December!* Oh well, there's a lot of moving to do! The house is *really* being done over; Daddy made his acceptance contingent on it. It should look really great when it's done!! Laurel goes into the Florence Crittendon ("home for unwed mothers"!) in Blue Hill tomorrow morning to take some test analysis to see if she *really* is pregnant. [She never found out with certainty; perhaps the fetus was spontaneously aborted.] Should be fun. Then when we get back to Melrose, she has to go into Boston for all sorts of examinations. Am I glad I'm not her! I wouldn't be able to go through with it! But luckily for her, she's not like me that way.

Before she left Maine that summer, Vivienne wrote this last poem:

> *It's my place to know*
> *Consistent emptiness and loss*
> *Within my soul.*

> *It is my place, also*
> *To know Joy just before it vanishes*
> *And sorrow just before it appears*
> *Within my soul.*
>
> *In my state of emptiness and loss,*
> *I live in the past*
> *In what is beautiful and with grace*
> *Never living today*
> *Which will soon be past and*
> *Never present again.*
>
> *"I seek you, to make me live the present*
> *Which will soon be past"*
> *This I say*
> *From within my soul.*

By the end of August, David had decided to take the ministry in Gloucester. The family planned to move in December.

"I had decided to go, but I was torn. I kept going back and forth in my mind. It was hard to leave Melrose. We had good friends there. The parsonage in Gloucester needed repairs. I told the church I wouldn't move in until it was ready to live in." There was no definite moving date.

There was an even more serious decision in David's mind. Should he stay in the ministry? Did he actually want to go into another career? These questions motivated David to seek pastoral counseling. It was decided that eventually the whole family should go to these meetings. Appointments were to begin in September.

Cambridge School started in early September. Vivienne and Laurel arrived, excited but somewhat shy newcomers. In one of her initial English classes, Vivienne met Anne Tucker.

"I think it was her first English paper that she read aloud in class," Anne said. "It was about suicide. I had a special interest in that because my older sister had taken her own life in August, right before school started. I think I was like a survivor to Vivienne."

Anne and Vivienne were close friends immediately. Anne is a feminine young woman, with round, questioning brown eyes and a full mouth that seems on the verge of smiling. She ponders questions thoughtfully, and speaks in bursts of words and hesitations. "We used to go on long walks around the campus," Anne said. "She told me all about the pills in August. I knew from what she told me that she was very, very serious about suicide, but it was sacred, like a secret between us. I could never have betrayed her by telling anyone. It would have been like stabbing her. I had no choice."

Anne wasn't the only one who felt that Vivienne's intention to die could never be shared. Laurel, too, ruled out her right to tell her parents or anyone else. "Sometimes she'd tell me that she'd tried to strangle herself," Laurel remembers. "I'd say, 'Why did you do that?' and she would say she wanted to. It was just sort of her way of talking about pain. I didn't know what to do. She swore me to secrecy. It's hard to explain, but it was like a trade-off. She knew about things I was doing that our parents would never approve of, and I trusted her not to tell them. She trusted me too." The respect for personal privacy was a firm unspoken rule among all the Loomises.

Vivienne gave her parents few clues about the depth of her depression. They knew nothing of what she was writing to John May or telling Anne and Laurel. Also in September Laurel and Vivienne had been given routine medical examinations and questionnaires by the physicians who served the Cambridge School. These too revealed nothing troublesome.

At CSW Vivienne seemed to be an industrious and contented student. Her teachers remarked on her "consistency" and "thoughtfulness." "She had a good sense of humor" and laughed a lot, Anne remembers, and seemed, much of the time, a "well-balanced girl." "People respected her. I thought she was unique. She was so wise, articulate, and eloquent. She understood everything. She was the only one I could talk to about my sister. Other people acted scared or upset about it, but Vivienne wasn't like that. She was interested in what I'd been through. She saw a spiritual side to suicide. She used to tell me that suicide wasn't a sick act. People had reasons for committing suicide, and she respected that. I admired Vivienne so much. She was honest and sincere. It made her angry when people played games. Other people found her 'cute' and 'funny,' but I think she wanted to be taken more seriously."

The serious side of both Anne and Vivienne felt to them like separate identities. "We had two different personalities," Anne said, "one at home and one at school." Anne was cheerful and hardworking in her classes, but at home she felt lonely. Vivienne, too, felt alone at home. "She was actually afraid of the moods she got into at home." When they came over her she felt "like a robot," without control of her emotions. She seemed scared of being at home as "nothing distracted her from her depression when she was home."

Anne and Vivienne were both very absorbed in their depressions. "I think when you are fourteen life isn't so precious," Anne said. Their youth, Anne felt later, robbed them of "some kind of perspective on what the rest of our lives would be like. Time seemed so long to us — to get through a week, even a day! For Vivienne, her little world — where she was going to die — was separate from everything else. We would go into this little world together."

Vivienne's schoolwork did not reveal a sense of pointlessness, but depressive themes and images can be seen in retrospect. In her English classes, she used assignments imaginatively. In October the class was asked to write a paper on a dream. Vivienne wrote a sensitive, well-expressed story, rich in obscure childhood memories and haunting symbols of death. A poem inside the story hints at her anticipation that her own soul would never find its fulfillment.

October 8, 1973

ON RECOGNITION

The alleyway is nothingness except for the brick walls on either side, that move closer to meet each other. I enter it, because it is here that I meet the night. Lowering my head, I will try to ignore the stars, which compete with the moon for brilliance, over me.

The hours of a life-time turn slowly in my head. My grandfather comes back to me now, with his intensely gentle eyes and a strangely distorted face. An unconquered mind; I remember he always used to tell me that my ~~dear you must never forget in all your life that eyes are for seeing and~~ *dreams* were for pursuing. He is with me now, and he paints me his pictures of flat-tailed doves that glide purposefully over black and scrawny ravens who fight over death. And he shows me carefully, the valley where the two mountains of reason and emotion meet and twine their efforts together in winding streams that quietly defy your logic. But just as I relinquish my power to fight this strange current, and I feel the waters rush through my veins, my grandfather is leaving me ... to remember.

... I flatten myself against the walls and ground around me, almost as if I know what is about to happen. Because soon I can hear them in the blackness; noisy and squabbling amongst themselves. The next thing I know, they are trampling me down. It feels so raw; I can watch their faces over me. There's my old nurse who used to sit for me, and my first boyfriend ... so ignorant and oblivious, with such cheap ideals. The cracker-jack-soul-jazz piano player who played at the corner bar, the little girls with ribbons in their pony [pig ?] tails, the candyman (he used to deal just down two streets from me), the tough-toed hockey players. My first lover. So blind, they can't see. ... Not even me! as they unite to grind me to the ground. But they pass as a storm and leave me there, just whole, to nurse my shredded existence. And it *does* heal, gently and gradually, making peace with the world.

But excuse me, for letting my mind wander like this. I don't mean to bore you. You know, sometimes I do this: my dreams become real, and reality becomes nothing but a dream. It's all so absurd. My friends are always telling me that I'm insane, but I don't *feel* like some kind of mad-man that should be behind bars. What do you think?

So now I'll get out of this dingy alleyway. I'll go talk to the street cleaner. But as I stand talking to him now and everything is supposed to seem so super-ordinary, he hands me this piece of paper from out of the gutter! Let me read it to you — see if you can understand it.

> *A star unlit*
> *A child unborn*
> *The tear inside*
> *The cry. These things*
> *Shall make you free.*

I know there is a sun
Before daylight,
And I am certain that
The flower lives
Before it ever blossoms;
That there is a soul in me.

> *A star unlit*
> *A child unborn*

> *The tear inside*
> *The cry. These things*
> *Shall make you free!*

My God! You know? I *do* understand this! My grandfather's dream! . . . Everything that I've told you has been in the wrong order! It's exactly like the poem, only in the wrong order!

The stars and moon that I never would allow to light up, those are the stars unlit. And the stampede of faces in the alley — those are the children unborn. The tear inside, the cry, that is my grandfather, the core of his dreams. The pictures he painted for me were the sun and flowers, then it all resolves again as the street cleaner releases me from this strange hold and sets me free in sudden recognition through all of this. To know and understand the night has set me free.

A few days later, Vivienne responded to an assignment on propaganda with an ironic and sophisticated parody.

October 11, 1973

BLOCK B

PROPAGANDA

The following is an editorial sent in by Mr. Garrett to the *Manchester Union Leader;* "A Message to My Fellow Responsible American Citizens."

Of increasing aggravation to the American public is the "American" Indian. This foreign minority exists purely off the fat of our land. They are rebellious tyrants who are ungrateful for our fine generosity. Trying to follow the established code of "forgive and forget" becomes increasingly hard for our government. America, no doubt, will reach the end of her rope and these uncouth troublemakers will be forced to take their exit.

When our first Americans tried to settle down and make a home of their newly founded country, I am afraid that the Indian had formed a rather cock-eyed view of what a welcome-wagon should be. They were wild animals; putting sharp and poisoned arrows through men, women and children alike. They introduced a new horror to the lives of our civilized fore-fathers — by scalping (alive, many times!) the heads of their victims. They performed ludicrous slaughterings on our trusting and kindhearted ancestors.

And yet, perhaps unwisely, one *begins* to think, we have tried to forgive them; we have left plenty of room for them to live normal lives amidst our rich and plentiful country. We have given them boundless opportunities to better their lives: a good, solid education, true religions, a stable and civilized government to live under, fine jobs and nice homes on lovely land.

... When the government decides after some deliberation, that it is best to run a highway through an Indian reservation, there is always a big ruckus put up by the red-face. Now obviously, we have put the highway there as a simple, practical convenience to the modern society of today. It is *ridiculous* for a tribe of half-witted trouble-makers to storm about disturbing important people by telling us that we are uprooting a cluster of old shacks leaning against each other in the middle of nowhere! ... We can curb our tempers. However, ultimately the responsibility lies heavily on the Indians if they wish to co-exist with America. Until the Indian as a people can learn to live harmoniously within the laws of this government, we can spare little sympathy for them.

Thank you,

Mr. Garrett

Vivienne wrote her first impressions of her new school to John May on October 14. The letter gives no indication of the stress that both Anne and Laurel were noticing. She described her courses, mentioned the family move now planned for early or mid December, and asked how he was doing with his five freshman classes.

Three days later another chatty letter followed that revealed how much she missed CFS. It began with a visit back to CFS and provided news of teachers they had both known. The letter continues:

> It's hard to get used to having your whole life become so much less personal all of a sudden. Which is the difference in the change from Friends to Weston. It's not that Weston is so *impersonal*; it's that Friends was so *extremely personal*. I miss it.

In the rest of the letter Vivienne told about her grades ("B in everything . . . because I didn't sweat my brow for any of the courses and I should have"). It was the first time she had gotten grades in three years and she complained of the "added pressure." She praised the music department and said she was taking flute lessons for the fourth year. She asked him for the names of books she might read as "you know my tastes" and "our books are all packed up so I can't get any here."

The letter concludes:

> When you do find the time, please write and tell me how you are surviving your five freshmen classes and how everything is with you. Those kids make me green with envy. They don't know how lucky they are to have you as their teacher. (But you should know *that*.) I hope all is fine.

> > With much love,
> >
> > *Vivienne*

At the end of October, Vivienne wrote another cheerful letter to John that was never mailed. It was found in a school notebook after her death. She wrote of designing a silk-screen poster for school, using a favorite quote, "Do not go gentle into that good night." The letter continues with news of her singing in two Melrose church choirs and tells of a new black-and-tan puppy named Tigger, but "we're not sure if we will actually be *keeping* her because she's such a menace."

In November Vivienne wrote two poems, which reveal her recurring depression, hopelessness, and loss. The first was a new one, but the second was a rewritten version of a poem she had composed earlier.

> November 4, 1973
>
> *Resigned*
> *Compromised and rehearsed.*
> *Striving to please*
> *The friend of the family:*
> *Don't go near*
> *The unknown child*
> *So sweet and wild . . .*
> *Wise and mild.*
>
> *Live their lives:*
> *Cling to what's left*
> *After the sequin suns*
> *And shiny metal money.*
> *Leave their regrets*
> *On answering service*
> *And the little ones*
> *Blinded by the glare.*
>
> *One time,*
> *Survive, place of soul*
> *To escape.*

Once for a lifetime yours,
Solitary;
The simple peace
From common crowds,
Bloody knives.

AND WHERE IS THE MOON?
You have taken the sun
And where is the moon?
(They think I'm too raw
When the stars go out.)
No more brilliant gifts:
I have nothing to shine
On your face, in your eyes!

So I turn for the moon
That echoes between the trees
A bitter shimmer, perhaps:
What reflecting waters conceal ...
... There is no sanctity here!
There is nothing!

God help me!!
... There is nothing.
Nothing.
And you have taken the sun
And
Where
Is the moon?!

CAMBRIDGE SCHOOL OF WESTON
November 12, 1973

It wasn't until a Sunday night in early December that Vivienne let anyone know how troubled she was and that the situation was serious. It was again to John May that she wrote.

She mentioned for the first time that the family was having counseling. This was an outgrowth of David's questioning of his future in the ministry. Although it had been originally scheduled for September, it had taken longer to find an appropriate pastoral counselor and the meetings did not begin until early November. The sessions were weekly and were attended initially by the parents, Laurel, Rob, and Vivienne.

The pastoral counseling was not especially focused on Vivienne's problems. "We felt that the thing was to focus on us as a group and try to work out all the relationships," Paulette said. Later, the parents felt it would have been better for Vivienne to have had her own person to talk to.

Vivienne resented the sessions and thought they were stupid. She took a dislike to the counselor himself. According to Laurel, Vivienne would "close right up" in the meetings. Once when asked a question she got upset and cried and did not want to talk about anything. Mostly she sat silently and said nothing. Suicide was never mentioned.

"She was physically there at every meeting," Paulette said, "but she wouldn't talk. I remember one meeting, Vivienne suddenly started to cry. None of us could reach out and touch her. We all kind of looked at her. The therapist said, 'You are really hurting,' and asked her, 'What would you like from the family?' And she said, 'Understanding.' 'Which member of the family do you most want understanding from?' the therapist asked. And she said, 'Daddy. I want Daddy to know me.' When we got home that day I said to her, 'Honey, I would like to get to know you,' and Vivienne said, 'You wouldn't like it if you did know me.' Later Laurel told me she meant I wouldn't like it if I knew she was planning to commit suicide."

Vivienne again turned to John May. She wrote him of her sadness and made a cavalier reference to hanging herself. While she sounded lonely and depressed, the letter was not critically alarming.

Sunday night
December 2, 1973

Dear Mr. May,

I thought I'd surprise you with an unexpected letter.

Things have been going fairly roughly lately, but I suppose that I will have to pull through this time whether I like it or not. We will be moving on the 28th of this month: three days after Christmas. Rob has a room in Revere on the top floor of the day camp center for welfare kids. He'll be living there probably until next fall when he goes back to school. Laurel is her usual self (the world is in love with her). Mommy and Daddy are weathering this point in time fairly well, all things considered. We are having counseling for the family. I know that I am probably the most destructive factor, but it's a little late for me to say that. Once you said you were glad I was born. Now I have my doubts about the whole thing. If I didn't have to worry about Mommy and Daddy, I wouldn't bother finishing this letter before I hung myself. But I have to stick with them. Sort of like one burden holding up another, which isn't too stable a thing to begin with. For one thing, I haven't got a single friend nearby. As a matter of fact, I *have* only *one* friend to speak of at all, and she lives in Belmont. With the gas shortage I see her solely at school. I could do with a lover, too; I'm beginning to think that being "blinded by love" and living in a hazy world where everything is rosy and beautiful (if more or less false) might not be such a bad idea.

An immediate problem is that there is no place to go. Have you ever had that feeling? I don't even know what I want any more from anybody or anything. I wonder if you can tell that I've been crying all through this letter. I'm trying to make it as smooth as possible. The funny thing is that crying isn't even a form of letting go anymore. It's just sort of a routine thing like taking orange juice and toast for breakfast every morning. I mean, the pressure is there afterwards, all the time; it doesn't really matter what I do. It's strange living with no relief for so long.

I wish you were here. Just to be here. You were my very best friend; you still are (not that you've got any competition).

Maybe you could write me sometime. I don't know what you would say to this crazy letter. If worse came to worse, you could always ignore it and write about your teaching, which I would very much like to hear about.

I almost forgot to tell you. One of my poems may be going into the literary magazine at school. It's not very good at all but if *they* don't know that, I won't tell them. So we'll see if it comes out.

I think I'll end this now. I don't think that I have anything else to say. But thank you for reading this somewhat irrelevant letter.

Yours with a lot of unused love,

Vivienne

P.S. I meant to ask you all about how you are. (I haven't got any manners at all.)

In the last three weeks of her life Vivienne wrote several poems. By this time her despair was deepening dangerously.

I

Karram
The wind shall scatter them
Ten thousand times.

Passive assent
Is less than living
When rage
Is half of life.

The day has splintered
One thousand pieces
Beyond recognition.
And nothing more shall be.

Life is lost in dried flowers;
Brittle and faded stars
Have lost their riches
The winds have scattered.

2

Do you love me any more?
Are you there?
You know I need you.
Whose name can I call out?
Would anyone come running?
Because you know I need some one to love me.

3

If it hadn't been for the storm
On the last day of my time
Then perhaps
It shouldn't have been struck down
So cruelly.

It was early evening
With an afterglow still in the sky
And five gulls
Fighting routinely over some prize.
... When everything turned to dark.

The sky was low,
Deep gray and rumbling
~~In high strung~~
Tension on the verge of snapping

Vivienne talked with Anne a great deal about death and her wish to die. "We used to talk about death as something calm," Anne recalls. "I remember when my sister died, someone who saw her said that she looked peaceful. Peaceful! I pictured her sleeping and that was a comfort because she had been so unhappy when she was alive. She looked calm, they said. Vivienne and I used to talk about it like that, like it was a beautiful dream. I never could have considered it myself because I saw what it did to my family. But Vivienne just said she wanted to get out of it. I knew what she meant. I wanted to get out of it too." But in "a very basic way" Anne did not really believe that Vivienne would kill herself. "I could not think to myself that she would actually die." Anne knew, of course, of the various family problems and tensions and that she had lost in John May someone that she really admired. But none of these factors, she observed correctly, seemed to warrant such despair.

What Vivienne most wanted "to get out of" was her unbearable pain and depression. On Sunday, December 7, she tried once more to strangle herself. Anne said Vivienne told her of at least five attempts in all. Four days later Vivienne wrote to John May describing this attempt. As it turned out, Vivienne couldn't find an airmail stamp in the house and the letter didn't get mailed until December 19, two days before her death. John received the letter the day after Vivienne died. The letter began innocently. Although seriously suicidal by now, she said her depressions were episodic. She was still able to think about him and how he was getting on.

December 11, 1973

Dear Mr. May,

Here it is! In this very letter is enclosed a *Carrot Cake* recipe!! (You *do* remember the Carrot Cake recipe, don't you?) I hope that you enjoy it.

I really can't remember what, if anything, I told you in my last letter (did you get it? no great loss if you didn't). I have one good friend at school named Anne Tucker who lives in Belmont. She is going through, if anything, worse times than I am. Her sister committed suicide last summer (she was seventeen) and her closest friend died of heart failure a few weeks ago (she was only ten). Anne is the only person I told after I tried to — I guess you'd call it — strangle myself last Sunday night with a silk scarf. It sounds even *less* absurd than it was. Mostly because, although it only came on me in a sudden extreme depression (a time span of about fifteen minutes), it was planned out too thoughtfully.

... My parents were surprised to see me home so soon. I told them that I wasn't feeling well and went upstairs. And then it just happened. Even though I have gone over and over suicide in the last three months or so and developed what I would consider a logical and socially acceptable attitude on the matter, it all seemed to leave me in a second. I happened to be standing by my mirror. I looked at myself with a sort of wince, and then, almost mechanically, my hands stretched round my throat and centered in for what seemed a long while. And then the ringing in my ears stopped and everything became soft and hazy and I could just make out my head in the mirror, like a separate, bloated object. I started swaying (with no rhythm to it) and I fell into my bedpost and boxes on the floor etc. Unconsciously, I put out my hand to steady myself, and in so doing, started up my circulation. This in turn started me jolting uncontrollably, while still swaying I caught hold of the mirror and my jolts sent the mirror crashing against the wall. KRSHSH KRSHSH! again and again. As soon as I could I stopped it because it was so loud. Then I went through my sister's drawers til I found a long silk scarf. I tucked it up my sleeve so you couldn't tell that it was there and left a note by my bed that said *something* like "I didn't want you to think that it was because of you when it was only me all the time." Then I went downstairs and told Daddy I was going for a walk, for a short walk. He said "You'll be back soon?" And I said "Yes" even though I had no intention of it. Then I walked three blocks to a public park (because I didn't want anybody to have the worry of a dead body on their property). A lot of people got raped and mugged there, but I figured it would probably give them a good scare to do it to a dead body. It was *very* cold out, but I didn't pay any attention. I took out the scarf and wrapped it tightly around my neck and pulled as hard as I could — I was standing in the shade in case car headlights should pick me up from the road. The first couple of times were like with the mirror (everything soft and hazy — the traffic would slowly fade away to nothing) and I would eventually fall. It was weird because I could *see* the glass on the ground, but I couldn't feel it at all. And then I would try to get up, but I would be jerking too spasmodically and it would take me several minutes — while all the time I was afraid somebody would come by.

Finally I got it so I was cutting off the air completely and not just the blood. But then my lungs would just about burst and I would let go. After a while I knew the whole thing was useless and rather despairingly resigned myself to all the many tomorrows looming up ahead of me. I said "goodnight" to the trees and ground around me and walked back home. My father asked me "How was your walk — feel any better?" "Sure." "Yuh.... Sometimes a little fresh air helps..." I could have screamed if I'd had the energy.

The whole thing was as silly, infantile and above all as *futile* as everything else I could be doing with my life.

The thing about Anne is that she understands and feels these same feelings of loneliness, separation, peace and inner riot that I am constantly feeling. In the end we just sort of hold each other up from day to day. *You'd* like her: she's got the kind of personality you'd like to watch living. She really is one of the most fantastic people I've ever known. I wish you knew her — you can't describe somebody like that and do them justice.

Thank you for wading through this rather long account of one night. I thought I'd let you know what happened after that letter. It worries me that I have such terrific depressions from the middle of nowhere.

... If you want to, write me and let me know how you are getting on. I care about you, you know.

I'm going to try to make something for you for Christmas, if I can, and send it to you. Just maybe I'll get myself collected enough to put together a package for you. I hope so.

I hope all is well with you and that the teaching is working out. I know you're over there somewhere giving yourself to so many people just like when you were over here. It's hard getting used to teachers whose policies include avoiding getting personally involved with their students. This is more of a dog-eat-dog world every time I turn around again. I know there must be more people like you around here *somewhere;* maybe I should put out a "Wanted" ad. Well, this whole letter shows you just how depressed I am. But I'm not always like that. Write me back a really positive letter and tell me somewhere in it what an ass I am for writing people letters like this. (This whole thing reminds me of something like an episode of "Diary of a Mad Adolescent.")

Take care, with love,

Vivienne

John did not know what to do when he received this alarming letter. He knew Vivienne and her family were seeing a family counselor and thought her problems were being handled there. He felt resentful that her parents could not give her more. He wrote a supportive letter he hoped would sustain her.

When Vivienne returned to school on December 10, the Monday after her strangulation attempt, she told Anne about it. While Anne understood, she was upset.

"She told me that she got into this calm frame of mind when she was like that. She had thought of jumping in front of a car, but she didn't want anyone to have to feel guilty about killing her. So it wasn't an impulsive thing. She was really planning it. I was still grieving over my sister and over a little retarded girl I had helped care for. She was only ten and had died recently. So when Vivienne told me about trying to strangle herself, I said, 'I really can't take this if you do it!' I didn't want to hear about it. I think her depressions scared her. They scared me too, but I understood how she felt."

School ended for Christmas vacation on Tuesday, December 18. "I think she decided it was all over on Friday," Paulette said. "I noticed that between Tuesday and Friday she spent a lot of time reading her writing and her journals." The family was now set to move the day after Christmas.

"We were very much involved in other things," Paulette said later. On Thursday, December 20, Vivienne and Laurel wanted to go to a Christmas revue of traditional songs and dance, *The Revels*, but their mother felt exhausted. Thursday evening Vivienne and Laurel went to choir practice. They visited a painter, a friend of several members of the choir. The girls were excited about the visit, but Paulette did not respect his work. "I think all of these things that weren't positive input were just making the vortex go faster," she said later.

On Friday night, while Paulette and David attended a farewell party and as Laurel played the piano in the living room,

Vivienne tied the rope on the water pipe in her mother's silver-smithing studio. She somehow fashioned the noose, and silently jumped to her death. It was a matter of minutes before Laurel came down to the basement.

The next morning Paulette found a poem on Vivienne's night-stand together with a note.

*I discovered and wrote this for myself three years ago —
but perhaps we all need to be reminded now and then.*

> *A star unlit*
> *A child unborn.*
> *The cry inside*
> *The tear. These things*
> *Shall make you free.*

I know there is a sun
Before daybreak;
I am certain that
The flower lives
Before it ever
Blossoms . . .
That there is a soul in me.

> *A star unlit.*
> *A child unborn.*
> *The tear inside*
> *The cry. These things*
> *Shall make you free.*

Vivienne

As Anne Tucker and her family were preparing for their trip to the West Coast, the phone rang. Anne answered it. It was David Loomis. He asked to speak to her father. "Suddenly I knew," Anne said. "Why else would he be calling? I was struck dumb. I thought it must be a dream. I thought she would come back to school after Christmas vacation. All I could do was cry. I couldn't talk to anyone. I wanted to go to the service. I wanted to be with the Loomises. But they made me go to California the next day. They thought it would be better for me."

As Anne was going to the airport, the day after Vivienne's death, Paulette found one last poem on the kitchen table:

> *When you are*
> *Too weary*
> *To go on*
> *And life strikes*
> *Such a finalizing chord,*
> *You have a choice.*
>
> *You can either*
> *Take your bow*
> *And leave.*
> *Or carry the tune*
> *Appreciating the crescendo*
> *As exactly that.*

Although John was unaware of it, he received Vivienne's letter the day after her death. He pondered an answer and wrote a long letter that did not reach the Loomis household until January 8.

Dear Vivienne —

My life is finally seeming settled enough to write. This has been a rocky fall for me. It was difficult to get back to full-time teaching after such a long break. It is also hard to teach in a public school system again where I have to work with 150 students a day and teach things I am not really sure even deserve the time. But I have come

through it. I don't think I'll be teaching forever at least
not in this current form (i.e. public school English). I am
feeling like I am doing a good job.

My life, otherwise, is also starting to take good shape.
(I've lost a little of my slender shape.) I start folk dance
lessons this Wednesday. Fran's and my relationship is
slowly becoming deeper and better. I have my own apartment in San Rafael with a beautiful view of a mountain.
I went to my parents for Xmas and then to a Co-Counseling Workshop in Santa Barbara. The workshop was
fantastic and a real growing event for me. I feel much
more in charge of my life.

I am glad to have gotten your letters. Please continue
to feel free to write me from whatever mood, realizing
all the time that I know what a great person you are. You
are one of my favorite people in the universe. Just the
knowledge of you often helps me in many ways. I must
comment on your depressions. You mentioned how you
appreciated my teaching and being; well, from one point
of view, you might say that the reason I give in the way
I do is so that I can in some way make the world an exciting and loving place to live. I expect and hope that the
students whom I have met on a more than "hello, turn in
your papers" basis are going to be around to be my friends.
I look forward to our friendship lasting for the next 60–
100 years. The sharing and enjoying of each other that
we can do during those years is exciting. Even 3,000 miles
apart our lives touch in letters, but also in thought. Stay
around!

I have turned my "I'm gonna write at least one letter a
week" leaf over so often that it is almost too worn to
turn but this is at least a beginning. . . .

. . . Remember that I love you — OK?

Love —
John

The day after Vivienne's death, Paulette had to make some immediate decisions.

"I had to think right away," Paulette said. "I could have called it an 'accident,' but I decided there was only one way and that was to be truthful. Here I was going to be an example to the other children. If I tried covering up then they would see that their mother was going to cover up and their father was going to say it didn't happen. . . . The only way was to say exactly what happened."

The memorial service for Vivienne was held on December 26. It was conducted in David's church in Melrose. The ushers were six young men who had been Vivienne's friends. The organist, Lee Colby Wilson, was a special and important friend and teacher to the Loomis children, particularly Rob and Laurel. Vivienne's poetry was used in the service as was a treasured passage from Ralph Waldo Emerson that Vivienne had done in calligraphy once as a present for her mother. Her favorite hymn, "Turn Back O Man," was the final musical offering.

Everyone who had known Vivienne felt the terrible silence of her leaving. "I didn't want it hushed up," Paulette said. "I wanted her life to mean something. I wanted other young people to know she shared their pain. But I wanted them to find a different answer. Vivienne was by far the best thing that ever came to this family. It can be put aside. But it can never be forgotten."

Two months after her death John May wrote to the Loomis family:

February 14, 1974

Last night I went to my folk dance class and, as it seems to happen so often, I thought of Vivienne. Near the end of the evening they did the Salty Dog Rag and I remember Vivienne . . . doing that dance. . . . But the dance that I danced for, with, and thinking of Vivienne, was an Israeli dance called the At-va-ne (you and me). I don't know if you've ever seen it but it's one of the loveliest and gentlest of folk dances. Its softness always touches me as did Vivienne's gentleness. She was a *jewel* and I am extremely thankful for the fact of her being in my life.

I, too, am caught unawares by flashes of memories of her and deep grief. It seems so unfair, but then that was the only way she saw to relieve her pain.

You are right. I do have times of *remorse* for my lack of writing. One of the sad ironies was that the last letter I wrote to Vivienne was the beginning of a writing-a-letter-a-week resolution which I have been very faithful to. I have been trying to work through my grief and have cried many tears (I am thankful for co-counseling). Some of the things that seem to be coming clear for me are that I must continue to cry and remember how wonderful it was to know Vivienne. That she will continue to influence my life. I believe in my last letter to her I said that I felt her touch my living even though we were 3,000 miles apart and now even if we are apart in other ways, she will still be part of me. That I must take care to care effectively for those whose lives touch mine, and that Vivienne made a choice, which grieves us all, but it was the only one she saw . . .

TWO

Meanings

JOHN E. MACK

A Clinician's Analysis

The Solution of Suicide

AS SUICIDE has lost the sense of sin with which it has been associated in Judeo-Christian cultures, the choice of ending one's own life has become increasingly available as a resolution of intolerable emotional pain and conflict. Walker Percy wrote in *The Last Gentleman* that when it loses its sinfulness, "the nurtured possibility of suicide" makes death "the very condition of recovering oneself." [1]

The decision to end one's life is an ultimate statement of that life's perceived worthlessness and possibly of the worthlessness of human existence itself. It is a choice that reaches to the core of human values and purposes. James Carroll, a former Paulist priest, wrote in his spiritual essay *The Winter Name of God* that neither "religious moralism which sees suicide simply as *sin*" nor "the moralism of psychology which looks at it in terms of *pathology*" is sufficient; "suicide, considered directly, opens us to the very mystery of existence. It is a revelation of the quality of human freedom and the transcendence to which it points." Albert Camus once wrote, "There is but one truly philosophical problem, and that is suicide." [2]

Jean Baechler, Francine Klagsbrun, and others who have studied suicide, stress — correctly, I believe — its complexity and the futility of attempting to reduce the problem to simple causes. Joseph Teicher and Jerry Jacobs emphasize the importance of examining the "total biography" of a suicidal adolescent so that, as Baechler wrote, "each variable may be assigned an intelligible place within the whole and with respect to other individual variables." [3]

As we reconstruct Vivienne's life and death in the effort to understand her decision, it is important to bear in mind that the selection of material for this purpose will, inevitably, give a skewed picture of Vivienne as a person. Although it is her depression and death that have led us to write of her, there was much in Vivienne that was lively and healthy, above all her humor and the capacity for fun. In a later section the question of prevention among adolescents who are suicide-prone will be considered. One can see, however, from Vivienne's case, how difficult the problem can be, how deep and complex are the elements that determine the ultimate outcome.

Children in early adolescence rarely talk about their deepest feelings and conflicts. Vivienne in some respects was not an exception. She could, like quite a few adolescents, more easily write of her thoughts and emotions. She speaks articulately through her diary notes, poems, school compositions and letters. Peter Blos, a pioneer investigator of adolescent psychology, observed that "a teenage girl is particularly likely to share her secrets with her diary as with an intimate confidante. . . . Daydreams, events, and emotions which cannot be shared with real people are confessed with relief to the diary." Because they reveal so much of their fantasy life and emotions, Blos wrote, "the study of adolescent diaries is of great interest, even if we have not other knowledge of the diarist. . . ." [4]

Diaries and other documents fill in many ways the gap that mental health professionals generally encounter when they try to fathom the inner world of a seriously suicidal adolescent. But as sources they are limited, for we cannot follow up the directions they furnish with our many questions.

Rob described his family as being "always a little bit different." The Loomises were reformist Protestants in Catholic neighborhoods; liberals among political conservatives. Laurel conveyed the Melrose community's objection to the family: "We weren't tight laced. We went to Europe; we had foreign cars. The neighbors thought we were Communists. Rob had long hair. I never wore a bra. [Sometimes] I didn't go to church.... I didn't go to Sunday school. I didn't just go and hold out May baskets on May Day." [5] Later in her growing personal isolation Vivienne could find no comfort or support in the community where her family experienced such alienation.

From early childhood Vivienne experienced the contradictory nature of her parents' personalities and the tension between them. Her father was consistently deeply moral, a man of convictions and integrity, yet indecisive and ultimately self-sacrificing. He seemed to Vivienne unable to hold his ground against "the common crowds and bloody knives." The mother was dominant in the family and ambitious for creative achievement, wishing to make something that would last two thousand years. She focused these needs on her children, especially upon Vivienne, who seemed to her to be artistically precocious.

Paulette felt her distance from Vivienne from the beginning. The delivery-room experiment seems to have set the stage for their alienation. Substituting music for anesthesia, and permitting crowds of hospital personnel to observe the results, Paulette seemed as much to be launching the creation of a work of art as giving birth to an infant. Paulette believed that the first disharmony between mother and daughter occurred when Vivienne contracted jaundice as a result of the mixing of their "incompatible blood types."

As is most often the case in disturbances of early mother-infant bonding, the "tuning out" that Paulette describes in Vivienne seems to have been mutual and reciprocal. Burdened with two "live wire" older children, Paulette was grateful at the time that Vivienne demanded little attention as an infant, was quiet and could be left for long periods to play alone in her playpen. Later, Paulette felt Vivienne had been injured by being left alone so much.

At two Vivienne's response to her mother after the ten-week separation seems to reflect the early alienation between them, and by three she pitted herself against her mother with an intense stubbornness. By age four and a half Vivienne had already developed the sensitivity that made her vulnerable to depression and suicide. She showed even then her unusual empathy for the suffering of others, her ability to identify with their pain. This tendency was first demonstrated in relation to her mother. Vivienne felt deep grief after the death of her maternal grandfather. She identified strongly with her mother's pain, which merged with her own sadness over the loss of this man they both had loved. Later echoes of this loss are expressed in the school essay "On Recognition," written two months before her death. Vivienne's empathy, her ready identification with suffering, would bring her later to experience diverse examples of human pain as if they were her own. Most compelling, however, would always be her need to assume her family's griefs and burdens. These two related aspects of Vivienne's development — the emotional injury in her earliest human relationships and the intense capacity for empathy with the pain of others — would leave her exquisitely vulnerable to loss and disappointment and, ultimately, to depression and suicide.

Vivienne's isolation from her peers in the Melrose elementary-school classes paralleled her parents' alienation in the town. Differences in style of dress and her unusual sensitivities set Vivienne apart from her schoolmates, and made her an object of derision. Her bookishness and biting humor deepened the gulf, and Vivienne was thrown back upon her family. Her intense fondness for her father, and the beginnings of her role as confidante to her mother, especially concerning problems within the family, emerged during these years.

Although Vivienne was alienated from the members of her community, and unable to discuss her feelings with her parents, her writings reveal a great deal about her emotional life, especially about her private struggle over the value of her existence. But these revelations explain incompletely her decision to die, and may leave us ultimately unsatisfied. Why did she view suicide as the only solution? Her writings identify factors, motives, determinants, but cannot in the end provide a complete explanation. As Alfred Alvarez has written, the motives of the suicidal individual are "devious, contradictory, labyrinthine, and mostly out of sight." [6]

Vivienne's Depression and Loss

In trying to understand Vivienne and the tragedy of her life there is no correct place to begin. One could start with her suicide and examine the specific meaning of her act. Or one might begin with an analysis of her personality, a consideration of her strengths and vulnerabilities. I have chosen to start with her depression, as I believe that this provides the best approach to understanding Vivienne's act. The suicide is a direct outgrowth of Vivienne's depression, while the depression in turn derives from the structure of her personality. One may move forward, so to speak, from the depression to the suicide, or backward from it to Vivienne as a person. From any perspective the depression is central. Yet for Vivienne herself the "terrific depressions" seemed to have a kind of independent life, to come at her as if "from the middle of nowhere."

It is important to recognize that the study of childhood and adolescent depression and suicide is relatively new, a development, really, of the past two decades. A great deal remains to be learned. Interest in the depressed states of children has of necessity followed the recognition of childhood itself as a period of human existence that is important in its own right and not merely a preparation for adult life. The greater attention given to children and their emotional problems, and the increased clinical sophistication that has followed from it, needs also to be kept in mind when evaluating statistics that show depression and suicide in childhood and adolescence to be increasing in frequency.

The recognition and understanding of depression in the young has been hampered by theories about adult melancholia, which cannot always be applied to children. Because their personality organization has not reached a level of complexity sufficient to fulfill the conditions of adult depressive states, so the argument has gone, children could not become depressed. There was truth in this argument, if the requirements of the clinical picture of adult depression were to be imposed on the child. In the past twenty years clinicians have increasingly realized that children and early adolescents have their own ways of showing depression, consistent with their level of development, but different from that of adults. Weepiness, sadness, unhappiness, boredom, withdrawal, physical complaints, failure in school, difficulty sleeping, changes in eating habits, sexual promiscuity, a tendency to have accidents, feelings of being unloved, abuse of alcohol and drugs, and suicide threats may all, for example, be expressions of depression, or what has sometimes been called "depressive equivalents," in childhood.

Although the pioneering work in depression of Sigmund Freud, Karl Abraham, Edward Bibring and Edith Jacobson was carried out with adults, it has nevertheless provided a basis for the understanding of depression in children and young adolescents. The work of these psychoanalysts has shown that continuing low self-regard is at the core of all depressive states, including those of childhood and early adolescence. The behavioral changes, or the expressions of troubled affect or mood, that are seen in childhood depression are a direct outgrowth of this lowered self-esteem. Because of the immaturity of personality structure, and the rapid developmental changes taking place, even in the depressed child, the clinical picture will fluctuate more in childhood than in adult depression. Similarly, the distinction between "depression" as a term to describe a state of feeling in contrast to its use to designate a diagnostic entity, clinical illness or syndrome, so important in thinking about adults, has less meaning when applied to childhood or adolescent depression. In the case of children and early adolescents the boundary between an affective state or mood and a clinical syndrome is blurred; and, in fact, they rarely show a picture of depression that could properly be called an "illness."

The reasons for this have to do with the variability or fluidity of children's responses to painful or stressful situations. They have rarely before the age of twelve crystallized the personally costly repetitive or fixed patterns of response that we call illness. Rather, they may react with withdrawal, a fall in school performance, rebellious activities, physical symptoms, irritability or other changes in mood or behavior that suggest the child is seeking to ward off the distressing feelings associated with lowered self-regard. By approximately age twelve, children seem to have developed sufficient intellectual capacity to assess their situation, and critical self-judgment to experience prolonged states of lowered self-regard that resemble in this respect the depression of adult life.

The picture of depression in adolescence begins to resemble adult depressive illness but has its own characteristics. The cardinal feature, the shifts of mood, is especially difficult to evaluate because of the tendency of some normal adolescents to be subject to wide swings of emotion and to experience times of feeling sad, down, "black" or "depressed" (a term which is rapidly becoming a cliché among teenagers). Other features, described by Carl Malmquist in his classic paper on childhood and adolescent depression, include unresolved dependency struggles (shown, for example, in difficulty developing a life separate from the parents or insatiable seeking of affection); chronic inability to feel satisfied with ideals, ambitions or self-concept; acting-out behavior such as sexual promiscuity, drug abuse, theft and violence; confusion of identifications (who am I like or would I wish to be like) and of identity (who am I, a loss of inner continuity); heightened self-doubting and condemnation.[7]

One of the findings in Vivienne's case, which seemed rather surprising to us, was the complex psychological structure of her depression that her diary, letters and poetry revealed. Child psychiatrists who have worked with adolescents have noted their limited ability to describe inner moods or personal conflicts. The child psychoanalyst Vann Spruiell, for example, wrote recently, "Perhaps there is no more mysterious time of life than early adolescence. Even adolescent patients rarely give us access to these aspects of inner life; adult analysands often cannot remember or their analysts are not interested. Normal boys and girls may tell each other some things, but it is safe to guess that their confidences are guarded and limited."[8] Vivienne, because of her ability to write articulately about her inner life, has given us many views of her emotional state and of the quality of her depression.

We may think of Vivienne's depression as being manifested in three fundamental dimensions: behavior, feeling and self-regard. These are interrelated realms, and the placement of a particular feature or personal expression under one or another of them is at times arbitrary.

One of the most striking aspects of Vivienne's depression was how little of it could be seen in her day-to-day behavior.

Her killing herself, Rob said, demonstrated "a thousandfold more than any indication she ever gave." With the benefit of hindsight one may go back and notice that she had difficulty making new friends at Cambridge School of Weston, or that the friend she selected was a girl whose sister had recently killed herself. Or we may observe that whereas she had always tended to be on the quiet or shy side, and to spend a good deal of time by herself, her isolation had increased in the last two years. Paulette, remembering, thought that Vivienne had become sadder, more withdrawn in the spring of 1973, soon after John May had left. She had also just read Sylvia Plath's *Bell Jar*. Although family members noted how moody Vivienne was during these last months, in their discussions with us no one ever fixed a point at which she seemed to change abruptly.

Vivienne's suicidal preoccupations and behavior were, of course, expressions of her depression. The only suicide attempt that came to her parents' attention — the pill swallowing in Maine — was noteworthy for its seeming superficiality, and served, if anything, to *distract* them from the seriousness of her depression, especially as they were so concerned with the possible pregnancy of their more actively rebellious daughter, Laurel. Vivienne had told Laurel and Anne Tucker of her desperation, and even of her suicide attempts. But they were sworn to secrecy and Anne somehow did not, or could not, believe she would actually kill herself. What is most impressive from the behavioral standpoint is not what Vivienne demonstrated of her depression, but, rather, how well she concealed its essential features.

Looking back through Vivienne's *written* communications an inner change seems to have occurred in November 1971 when she was twelve years and three months old. It was then, in conjunction with her awareness that John May would be leaving before long, that she first wrote in her journal of the loss of joy and about dying (see page 34). We know also, primarily from her writings, that Vivienne assumed the emotional burden of each family member's troubles. To a degree these were imposed upon her, but more fundamentally this assumption of the pain of others was a feature of Vivienne's depression whose antecedents could be traced back at least to the time of the deaths of her two grandfathers before she was five. She sought out, we should remember, Anne Tucker in her mourning. Vivienne, her sister and brother felt, seemed, like her father in his church, to sacrifice herself for the benefit of the family.

Vivienne did not reveal her pain to those around her. Her mother commented in retrospect upon Vivienne's tendency to cover her "terrible depression" with wit and with comic imitations. But Vivienne's writing revealed best her dark feelings. It was in her journal, and especially in the poetry, that Vivienne recorded her pain, the sadness and her sense of hopelessness about the future. It was here, and toward the end in the letters to John May, that she communicated her desperation and the experiences of loss and of being lost. It was in writings that Vivienne could express her loneliness, the longing for love, the tears, the images of destruction of her inner world and the forebodings of death.

Paulette Loomis recalled it clearly. "What was bothering her," she said, "was that she felt she wasn't anything." When John May first met Vivienne at eleven he saw then that she "did not think she was worth much." He set out to boost her self-regard and had great, if intermittent, success; Vivienne's writings abound with instances when she was feeling down about herself and became happy after hearing encouraging words from him. Anne Tucker did not understand why Vivienne had so little regard for herself. "It wasn't that home was bad for her," she said, "but it was that her own self was so bad." Anne said that Vivienne "felt herself lacking physically; I think she felt bad about her body . . . everybody thought she was funny.

Everybody thought she was cute ... she couldn't make people take her seriously."

In comparison with her friends Vivienne would find herself inferior. One girl, for example, "was always ten times smarter than me in everything. It doesn't do anything for my ego"; or "I have the constant feeling that I'm big and clumsy and sort of dense beside someone who is small, precise, brilliant and absolutely perfect."

Vivienne's conviction that she was a terrible source of pain for her parents was in large part a displacement onto them of her own self-hate. After the first effort to strangle herself in July 1973, she wrote John May, "I've decided to torture them and give it another year." After the family counseling began Vivienne wrote, "I am probably the most destructive factor." When she first began seriously to think of suicide Vivienne wrote in her journal, "What good to kill myself? How can you kill nothing?"

The close relationship between the loss of loved or highly valued persons and depression has been recognized since the publication of Freud's seminal paper "Mourning and Melancholia" in 1917. Subsequent observations have established that a loss need not involve actual death or permanent separation from a loved person to precipitate a depressed or melancholic state. Loss of affection from the love object may be sufficient to bring about a state of pathological grief. Severe disappointment, as in the case of school failure, the loss of a job, or the loss of a dream or a deeply cherished wish, seems to be sufficient. The common factor in each instance is a loss of self-esteem on the part of the depressed person. Indeed, Edward Bibring in 1953 defined depression as "the emotional correlate of a partial or complete collapse of the self-esteem of the ego since it feels unable to live up to its aspirations (ego ideal, superego) while they are strongly maintained." [9]

In the case of children and early adolescents, loss of a loved or loving person, especially a parent, has similarly been observed to precipitate depressions. Less well studied has been the effect of the loss of other important persons, such as siblings, grandparents, teachers or friends, or the impact of failure, disappointment and other emotional injuries. Malmquist has suggested that "repeated rebuffs or losses reaffirm to the child that an important object did not place worth on him and that he is dispensable." [10] But, as I have noted, profound losses of self-esteem can occur in children and early adolescents without the death or recent loss of a beloved person.

Just why loss of a valued person should bring a fall in self-esteem has been a subject of continuing interest since Freud wrote "Mourning and Melancholia." Freud, and many writers after him, stressed the part played by identification and internalization. By this is meant that as part of the process of mourning the bereaved person takes into his own personality qualities of the lost object. There is a tendency to internalize these qualities, especially the critical ones. These devaluing voices then become amalgamated with the superego, or self-critical part of the griever's personality. The resulting harsh self-criticism then brings about a fall in self-regard. Depression does seem more likely to follow a loss in cases where the lost object was ambivalently loved. The severe self-criticism, which brings about the lowered self-esteem, may be thought of as a kind of atonement for the hostile attitudes harbored by the bereaved toward the deceased in life and in death. This theory, although relevant to her case, does not, as we shall see, sufficiently explain the recurrent and profound disturbances of self-esteem from which Vivienne suffered.

The understanding of early adolescent depression, such as that suffered by Vivienne, thus depends upon an understanding of the development, sustaining and regulation of self-esteem. One of the purposes of this book is to discover how in this child's case her self-regard became so profoundly disturbed. Malmquist has written that "loss of self-esteem as a response to loss is not thought to appear until a structural division of mental activity [in other words, sufficient complexity of the mind] has been accomplished." [11] In Vivienne's case this structure had indeed been "accomplished," perhaps in some respects precociously. Those mental agencies having to do with standards or expectations (the ego ideal); with evaluation of how well these are being fulfilled (a function of the ego itself); or with self-criticism for failure to measure up (superego) were seen to be actively engaged by the time she was twelve or thirteen.

By age twelve Vivienne grasped how vulnerable she was to separation, and even perhaps that she was drawn to those who might leave her. "Why do I have to like the people that are with me the shortest time in my life?" she asked in her journal. "Sometimes I think it's not worth the let-down in the end." An interesting comparison may be made with what Anaïs Nin wrote in her diary at about the same age: "I have decided that it is better not to love anyone, because when you love people, then you have to be separated from them, and that hurts too much." [12]

During the last year of her life Vivienne experienced several important losses. After three years she graduated from Cambridge Friends, the school that had meant so much to her, and she found the change to Cambridge School of Weston hard to accept. "It's not that Weston is so *impersonal*," she wrote to John May; "it's that Friends was so *extremely personal*." In her last letter to him she wrote — revealing, not the school's policy, but her perception of it — "It's hard getting used to teachers whose policies include avoiding getting personally involved with their students."

She was also soon to lose the home she had lived in since age seven. Although the family had not fit in well in Melrose, the imminent move to Gloucester represented a loss for Vivienne of what was close and familiar. She wrote little of her feelings about the move, but her stubborn refusal to help with the packing, and of course the timing and location of her suicide, speak eloquently of its powerful impact upon her. Laurel described the effect of the move on the family: "That month was an awfully strange time too, just because we were moving; the whole house was uprooted — no one knew where we were quite going — we were leaving everyone that we knew — going to a completely strange place . . . the house was upside down — quite uncomfortable . . . things were in a state of flux, not where they were supposed to be." Anne Tucker too spoke of the move for Vivienne as "a big uprooting." There was doubt about how Vivienne would get to Cambridge School of Weston ("a long drag" from Gloucester, Anne said). Although Vivienne experienced no physical loss of a parent, Paulette felt that their preoccupation with the move pulled her and David away from Vivienne emotionally. "We were very much involved in other things," she confessed.

The most important loss for Vivienne was clearly the departure of John May. Well over a year before he left, Vivienne anticipated that she would feel deeply bereaved, and wrote that her "joy will be gone in a year." Vivienne's writings around the time of John May's departure link in vivid images, especially in the poetry, his loss and the perception of her lack of worth. Her world has crashed and no replacement will do ("Something lost / And never found"). Vivienne's dream "is drawn and closed"; "our imaginary life" is lost; death seems inevitable.

And yet one wonders how this can be. How can the loss of a teacher, no matter how beloved, precipitate such a profound lowering of self-regard? The departure of John May had a greater significance than his loss as a person. It struck at the core of Vivienne's psychological vulnerability.

Self-Esteem and the Ideal

Anne Tucker understood her friend's need to be perfect in everything. Her own sister, who had also taken her life, had been the same way. For Vivienne, Anne said, "If you weren't perfect then this was no good. You [had] to be a perfect person." Vivienne's brother and sister came also to understand the uncompromising nature of Vivienne's expectations, the ideal standards by which she took the measure of herself and everyone else. It is here, in the unyielding intolerance of imperfection, that one can begin to understand Vivienne and her final decision.

Low self-esteem was at the heart of Vivienne's depression. Self-esteem, as we have come to understand it from the work of Edith Jacobson and others, is the evaluation of the self in relation to the goals and standards that the individual carries within. High self-esteem is experienced when the self, as it is perceived by the judging capacities of the ego, comes close to fulfilling these standards. Conversely, low self-esteem results when a wide gulf is experienced between the perceived self and the ideal self. During her analysis with Otto Rank in the 1930s Anaïs Nin says he told her, "The cause of discord in the personality is usually the tragic disparity between the ideal goal of the individual, the image he creates of himself, and his actual self." [13] We will call the standards by which one measures oneself, the ego ideal; the imagined person one would wish to be like as a result of achieving those standards, the ideal object; and the ideal person one would wish oneself to become, the ideal self. Clearly these terms are closely related to one another in meaning.

All of us experience times of lowered self-regard when failure, disappointment or loss inform us that we have fallen short of our ego-ideal expectations. But ordinarily such experiences are transient and do not achieve the intensity or depths of mel-

ancholia. A realistic assessment of the self's value is soon restored. But there are some individuals — Vivienne was one of
them — who are depression-prone, are vulnerable to continuing
and painful lowering of self-regard. In order to understand
what leads to this special vulnerability it is useful to consider
how self-esteem is normally maintained.

Contributions are made to the development and sustenance
of positive self-esteem at each stage of childhood. A colleague,
Nancy Cotton, has divided the sources of positive self-esteem
into three strands.[14] First is the esteem of others, the message
conveyed to the infant and small child initially by the parents,
and later by siblings, peers and other adults, that he or she is
empathically loved and valued. Parental praise and approval, if
genuine, as well as appropriate limit-setting, will contribute to
the development of high self-regard. Gradually these attitudes
are incorporated into the child's personality. A core of good
feeling about oneself develops, which is more or less independent of the approval of others, although some appreciation and
external validation of one's value is important throughout life
for sustaining high self-regard.

The second strand is the experience by the child of real ac-
complishment, the pleasure or satisfaction in successful mastery
of tasks or activities he or she has initiated. The experience of
being effective or competent in areas the child designates as
important to his or her self-concept, whether physical attractiveness, athletics, intellectual achievement, or popularity with
peers, will contribute strongly to positive self-regard. Since
successful mastery or skillfully performed activity is likely to
bring praise from others, the first and second strands tend to
become intertwined.

The third strand, and the one that concerns us most in Vivienne's case, is contained within the child's personality or self.
It is the outcome of the evaluation the individual makes of
how well the self is measuring up to the ego ideal.

Susceptibility to the experience of low self-esteem can thus occur as a result of injury or developmental failure in relation to any of these three strands. The parents may have shown too little approval, or set expectations of achievement too high for the child to reach. Malmquist has written of families in which "acceptance within the family is conditional upon [the child's] successes." [15] Or vulnerability, which may be transient or potentially reversible, can result from a depletion in the capacities of the ego itself brought about by fatigue, injury, illness, or any outside influence that causes loss or weakening of its faculties. Another cause of vulnerability, and the one with which we are most concerned, occurs when there is disturbance in the development of the ego ideal so that its standards for the self and for the outside world are urgently felt but can never be achieved. This was Vivienne's problem. Vivienne had many personal qualities and abilities in which she might have taken pride and for which she had always received a good deal of approval. She had a rich sense of humor and a sharp wit, played the flute and sang and danced well. She was an excellent student and an accomplished writer for a child of fourteen. But the disturbances in the genesis of her ego ideal, to which we now turn, prevented Vivienne from enjoying these assets or from experiencing herself as having any value.

The infant is increasingly being recognized by developmental psychologists as a far more sophisticated, discriminating and capable creature than was once thought. He or she is nevertheless quite dependent on the parents for warmth, food, and for the relief of a variety of bodily discomforts and tensions. In addition, parents help create a state of well-being or good self-feeling through holding, playing with and interacting lovingly and richly with the infant. Pleasure in the infant, and a communication of its intrinsic worth, will be conveyed in affectionate holding and in facial expressions that show love and approval. But inevitably disappointments will occur, what Heinz

Kohut has called "the unavoidable shortcomings of maternal care";[16] the parents will leave temporarily or will fail to come when the baby cries. The baby will feel powerless to reverse the state of pain or unpleasure that results. It is out of this conflict, psychoanalysts have hypothesized, that the forerunner of the ego ideal begins to take shape.

It emerges from two interrelated currents of development, tied to self-love, or narcissism, and to the love of others, or object love. On the one hand the small child begins to develop fantasies of grandeur and magical power that directly contradict the reality of his helplessness. Such fantasies are comforting insofar as they protect the child from the hurt to his developing self-esteem that a realization of his actual limitations would occasion. At the same time the small child begins to abandon the exclusive focus on the self and its needs, which characterizes infancy, and begins to develop the capacity to love others, initially, of course, the parents, but also siblings, other children and adults. This initial love is highly idealized; the parents are perceived as possessing extraordinary value and power, in which the child may partake if he can become like them.

The ego ideal begins to form as a psychological structure within the self as a result of these two currents of development. Because of its emergence out of the disappointments of infancy and early childhood, the ego ideal will always retain a close link to narcissism, that is, to needs and wishes connected with the desire for love and to the power and value of the self. It is the compensation in a sense for the lost perfection of childhood; for the child, adolescent or adult may later, at least in imagination if not in reality, recapture that sense of infantile perfection that he imagines he once had (what John Murray has called the "Shangri-la" of early childhood) by bringing the developing self into perfect harmony with the ego ideal. Heinz Kohut has pioneered in the psychology of the self through the psychoanalytic treatment of adults who have suffered early childhood traumas to self-development. He has observed how closely tied are the early childhood relationships with the parents to self-love and self-regard. He has introduced the terms "self-object" and "idealized parent imago" in order to convey the intimate link between early attachments to the parents and need satisfactions of the emerging self. Kohut's concepts can be applied to Vivienne's developmental disturbance.

The interest of children in fairy tales, in kings and queens with magical powers, and in heroes and heroines possessing special abilities and permitted certain prerogatives, are early expressions of the need to find idealized objects in the wake of the initial disappointments with the parents. The idealization of teachers and of older siblings and other adults is a similar reflection of this need. Under normal circumstances the child gradually modifies these idealized images, and builds a stable ego ideal out of the internalization of the prized qualities of loved or respected individuals together with family and group values in order to create enduring values, standards or expectations for the maturing self. The ego ideal is the mental structure that emerges as a result of these identifications. Children, as we shall see in Vivienne's case, in whom the approximation to their ego ideal remains dependent on the real or imagined love of an idealized person are especially prone to lowered self-esteem and depression should this person, or his love, be lost. Even among adults, ego-ideal expectations may never become altogether "realistic" in the sense that they can necessarily be literally achieved. Some of the most creative individuals maintain internal standards for themselves and others of beauty, achievement, world peace or romantic love that provide a powerful motivational stimulus for the strivings of the ego but can never be more than partially realized. Religious ideals maintain notions of absolute good but are not expected to be achieved literally.

The level of self-esteem is to a large degree determined by

the ego's assessment of the self as it functions in conformity with the standards of the ego ideal. Vulnerability to lowered self-esteem can thus result from too exalted ego-ideal expectations, especially if these are unmodified by actual experience, or if the moral or self-critical faculty (superego) judges the self too harshly for failing to live up to the standards of the ego ideal. The experience by the child of hostility, the perception that she experiences hateful feelings toward parents or others whom her ego ideal tells her she ought to love, is especially likely to result in a lowering of self-esteem.

Ego-Ideal Formation in Adolescence and the Meaning of Loss for Vivienne

Although its precursors can be observed in early and mid childhood, the ego ideal as a stable, integrated structure of the mind takes shape during adolescence.[17] Puberty or early adolescence in particular is a time of rapid change and reorganization of the personality. The child's efforts to affirm her identity as a person distinct from the parents, her more realistic assessment of the parents' limitations, and the simultaneous need to find objects outside the family as models to idealize, or upon which to build a stable ego ideal, all contribute to a tendency of early adolescents to become disillusioned with the parents and to devalue them, at times unmercifully. It is also a period in which the child forms intense, sometimes passionate attachments, often largely in fantasy, to peers, teachers or other adults. These relationships, which may have profound meaning for the child, are at times dismissed too casually by adults as "crushes." Often these idealized love relationships seem to reflect a desire on the child's part to find once again the parent of early childhood experienced in the first stages in the development of the ego ideal. One of the important tasks for the adolescent is to achieve a shift from the primitive idealization and glorification of the self and the object (Edith Jacobson has called this the "wishful concept of the self") to the establishment of workable values and goals and a stable ego ideal.

Early adolescence is a period of especial vulnerability to emotional injury. Rapid bodily changes, especially those associated with puberty and sexuality, inspire shame and discomfort, and inevitable comparison of oneself and others with respect to size, attractiveness and capability in a variety of spheres. Increased sexual fantasy and desire, and cultural pressure for early experimentation before the child can handle the choices she is confronting, may lead to confusion and feelings of profound self-doubt, emptiness and fragmentation. The early adolescent has not yet established a permanent ego ideal or a realistic assessment of the capabilities and limitations of herself and others. She still identifies with parents whom she subjects to critical evaluation.

These are the vicissitudes that affect to some extent all adolescents. A degree of self-confidence carried over from middle childhood, more or less certain knowledge that she is loved, and a limit upon the extent to which the young teenager gives herself over to the childhood patterns of idealization, will usually carry her through until more mature ego-ideal and superego structures can form and stable self-esteem regulation can be established.

What heightened risks to the development and sustenance of self-esteem may take place in adolescence, when the earlier phases of development have not been passed through smoothly? Kohut postulates that if there has been a significant disturbance in the parent-child relationship, either through a failure of empathy or a traumatic loss before the age of three, the child will be left especially vulnerable to later injuries to self-esteem. The individual will then seek idealized parent figures in adolescence or adult life, not as part of the process of normal ego-ideal formation, but rather to replace something missing in the self. Because they are needed in order to repair fundamental injuries in the structure of the self, idealized objects will be sought with particular urgency. As a consequence, losses of these objects at critical times will bring about not merely a loss of self-esteem but terrible emotional pain, a sense of nothingness, and, potentially, a dissolution in the structure of the self.

Vivienne's journal documents her central preoccupation with the ideal from the time she was eleven and a half and possibly earlier. "Did anybody ever wonder how close they were to their ideal?" Vivienne asked at eleven years and eight months. Vivienne's parents were struck by the uncompromising intensity of this quest. Paulette told us of how pained Vivienne was at the failure of the parents to live up to her vision of the ideal, such as perfect sensitivity, understanding, generosity, friendliness, kindness, compassion, and so on. "She was trying to reform us," Paulette said. "She wanted us to have a perfect, idealistic family and a relationship that was really amazing. You know, unless you were God you couldn't be that. But she had this vision of the ideal people. And we didn't live up ... she was angry that her vision wasn't being acted on."

Vivienne's need to find perfection limited her ability to have friendships, thus ensuring her loneliness. "To be somebody considered by her for friendship," Paulette said, "you had to sort of be a little bit unusual and have a personal integrity and honesty.... She had an awful lot of demands for what she felt she'd be willing to give herself to." There seem to have been few friends with whom Vivienne felt she had achieved, even temporarily, the perfect warmth, intimacy and understanding she craved. The only friend of whom Vivienne spoke often to Anne Tucker was a girl from Cambridge Friends School whom she exalted. By comparison to herself, this girl was beautiful and everything she did was graceful. The quest for the ideal extended, as we shall see, to society and to the larger world around her.

Vivienne's early adolescent preoccupation with the ideal, and with her "idea of an ideal person," although latent within, seems to have been crystallized by the interest John May took in her after her arrival at Cambridge Friends School. He was the only one, she wrote, who treated her the way she wanted to be treated, who was "sincere, trusting, honest and loving. I love him for that." Her fantasy of a lifetime of love is expressed in the poem of June 16, 1971. In her journal (June 22) she protested that her family misunderstood the poem to mean "me," but Vivienne insisted that she had a broader, more abstract meaning in mind. She went on to assert that she could only "love the little bit of life that touches my ideal one."

Laurel, too, found John May to be an understanding teacher — "a real sweetheart," she called him — and she also felt her confidence boosted by talks she had with him. "The whole sixth grade loved John May," Laurel said. But among the children in this class it was only Vivienne who came to depend so totally upon him. With his departure she anticipated her joy would be gone. After he had left she declared, "I am worthless," and began to contemplate suicide. What do we know about Vivienne that can help us understand why this loss was so shattering for her?

Vivienne's parents were deeply committed to altruistic aims, such as community service, sharing, and thoughtfulness toward others. It was painful for them to see their moral standards reappear in Vivienne in a kind of caricature, merciless criticism of herself and others, a zeal for reform that caused her much anguish. Vivienne, born to parents who stressed sacrifice, ultimately, John May felt, sacrificed herself for the family. But this moral strictness would not, I believe, have resulted in suicide, had there not been a deeper injury.

John May, and others who knew the family, found much love, warmth and concern for one another among its members. But from the time of Vivienne's birth and infancy there was a failure of rapport, of empathy between her parents and herself.

As her mother said to us — and these remarks must be tempered by our knowledge of the guilt she felt — "She was injured. We did injure her. She was the third child — she was the quietest, and I had these two other very active children and she didn't get the attention that the other two got simply because she didn't demand it. Yes, she was injured. This was definitely true." Vivienne's extreme sensitivity to the separation from her parents at age two is probably one reflection of her injury. By age three, as her parents noted, she had "tuned us out." Her reaction to the losses of her grandfathers before she was five is more indicative of Vivienne's already developed *sensitivity* to injury and loss than it was traumatic in its own right. Of her three children, Paulette seems to have had a tendency to perceive Vivienne more than the others in terms of her own personal needs, as a treasure, "better than anything that ever came along in the family," the one to whom she turned with her burdens. Vivienne, recognizing this quality in her mother, referred to her as "My Little Princess." Vivienne's essay "On Vanity," for all its humor, shows her profound knowledge of relationships in which apparent intimacy has an egocentric basis. In the last weeks of her life Vivienne felt especially the weight of her mother's problems and needs.

We have glimpses of Vivienne's special closeness with her father, but he later acknowledged that he never really knew Vivienne or "where she was." Sweet and gentle, he was, nevertheless, indecisive, had difficulty handling his son, and surrendered much of the authority in the family to his wife. The empathy Vivienne felt for her father's hurt and disappointment, his agonizing over decisions, only deepened her own pain. It was his tendency to take on "all the problems of the world," as Laurel put it, "the bloody knives," that was the quality in her father with which Vivienne most clearly identified. He would speak in relation to his struggles with the church of having to "bow out," to "take this move," and Vivienne, in the poem she left at the time of her death, wrote of how one should "Take your bow / And leave."

The early elementary-school period was one of further injury and humiliation for Vivienne, who became an outcast among her schoolmates. The hurts of this period would not in themselves have been decisive, but they built upon the deeper damage to the self that had occurred during the earlier years.

The unhappy eleven-year-old to whom John May reached out in October 1970 was not hurt merely as a result of her miserable public-school experience. But when he found that by Christmas her spirits had remarkably improved, it must have seemed that whatever the injury she might have suffered, it would be repairable if she could be encouraged to feel more positively about herself.

But Vivienne's needs were of a different order. She was questioning the value of her existence in a more fundamental way as a result of a deeper injury to her developing self. Rob seemed to grasp the special depths of Vivienne's needs. What she had required, he thought, was "three nights a week to sit down with someone and be able to thrash through the deepest issues of human existence."

The "amazing" improvement in her spirits, which followed upon John May's caring and assurances to Vivienne of her value, depended on his actual and continuing presence. His blandishments, so generously and honestly given, became, once experienced, essential for Vivienne to the integrity and value of her self.

The pain connected with John May's departure was overwhelming. He had completed Vivienne's existence, had become essential to the structure of her self. With his loss she became nothing. Sensing perhaps the nature of her irrational response, he tried, according to the Loomises, to tell Vivienne that he was not perfect. But John had no way to grasp the essential part Vivienne's idealization of him had played in her development. As an imagined object of perfection he had become essential for her survival. Not long after John's departure Vivienne wrote to him, "I was just wondering if you would please send me something encouraging, positive, anything! for me to live on for a while. It's funny, but I've really gone to pieces." Her poetry is filled with images of things crashing down, and being torn apart, of storms and "smashed attempts," of rubble, and of "the shattered wreck of hopeless dreams."

Vivienne, Her Culture and the Impact of Sexuality

Among the tasks of adolescence the integration of the rapid changes of puberty, and the sexual tensions and powerful emotional longings that accompany them, must rank near the top. Both adolescent boys and girls need to develop sufficient comfort with and acceptance of the transformed bodies they are inhabiting to permit them to tolerate some closeness with the opposite sex, and to begin the experimentation in physical intimacy that, hopefully, will lead in the end to mature and gratifying sexual activity and relationships.

Both boys and girls must defend themselves against the revival of early childhood sexual ties to each parent that is stimulated by the hormonal changes of puberty and the heightening of erotic sensation and fantasy that accompany them. The young adolescent girl, while needing to maintain her close attachment to her father, needs at the same time to guard against the activation of incestuous feeling that may occur at puberty. At the same time she is struggling to separate from her mother and to defend against the regressive pull of the old dependent relationship of childhood.

Although the sexual rites of passage must in some way be undergone by all adolescents, family attitudes toward sex and early childhood experience can influence powerfully how each child will handle the developmental challenges that she or he encounters. Laurel felt that her parents conveyed contradictory messages to their children about sexuality. On the one hand they stressed a certain naturalness, an attitude of physical freedom toward the body, and sometimes walked around the house without clothes in front of the children. At the same time, they both seemed to have had quite sheltered upbringings, and to be awkward and stiff, though not severe or punitive, in their discussion of sexual subjects with the children. The mother in particular, often it seemed in spite of herself, had an anxious attitude toward sex. When Vivienne, at twelve or thirteen, tested her mother's attitude by suggesting that when she was eighteen her mother would permit her to sleep with a boy in the family house, Paulette remarked. "I don't think I'm going to change that much."

Recent research by Maj-Britt Rosenbaum, a psychiatrist specializing in human sexual development, has confirmed what everyone who has been around teenage girls knows: how critically important for self-regard is their physical appearance and the image they have of their looks and figure. Vivienne never seems to have been comfortable about her body and her appearance. In elementary school she was teased about her overbite. Also, she tended always toward being overweight. She would gorge herself on candy and other sweets and tended to be quite plump. Her journal records efforts to reduce her weight through dieting ("I'm on this new diet and so far it's been *two* days since I've eaten anything fattening," she reported on December 6, 1972).

When she was ten a rapid increase in the size of her abdomen resulted in a pelvic examination that was so traumatic she never again "wanted to go near a doctor who was going to explore those regions." At eleven Vivienne's menstrual periods began. Although she did not write explicitly about the meaning of the menarche to her, Anne thought that Vivienne had always "felt bad about her body." It is likely that the prepuberty trauma that Vivienne experienced at the hands of the doctor, in which her mother might have seemed to Vivienne to be implicated, made her slow to experience the vaginal area as a part of her body that could bring pleasure, and interfered with her ability to feel that it is good to be female, leaving her instead with a fear of sexuality in its physical sense. The model offered by her mother of a burdened and thwarted woman may also have made it difficult for Vivienne to conceive of herself as enjoying the female role.

Vivienne's way of handling the sexual aspects of puberty and early adolescence contrasted sharply with Laurel's. As a small child Laurel had been obedient, "like the angel of my family," helpful to her mother and her siblings. Yet she felt kept down, "definitely the peon in the house." Although she, like Vivienne, had felt out of place at the Melrose school, in the seventh grade Laurel began to wear nylons, lipstick and great dangling earrings and to put her hair up on her head. At that school, Paulette said, "The emphasis was all on sex." Soon after this Laurel began to experiment and to struggle actively against what she felt to be her mother's moralistic and guilt-provoking ways. Paulette, clearly challenged and offended, felt personally attacked, was openly critical, and called Laurel a slut, which only propelled Laurel into more rebellious behavior. Laurel was far more outgoing socially than Vivienne and was popular among their peers. She tried to help her and to include Vivienne in groups of her friends, and Vivienne depended upon Laurel for what mixed company she had. The suicide gesture on August 16, 1973, was precipitated by Laurel's determination to go off on a date without Vivienne. Despite the fact that Vivienne seemed at times to be tagging along as the somewhat overweight kid sister, Laurel's male friends sometimes made passes at her, nevertheless.

Vivienne understood the deeper emotional needs that Laurel

was trying to satisfy, and described their differences in her letter to John May of July 21, 1973. "I disapprove of what Laurel does," she wrote. "But you can't rule someone else's life, can you? You see, Laurel and I have got the same basic problem. We both are very lonely and seek human ties. However, she seems to be satisfied with the physical aspect, whereas I crave a more spiritual relationship where physical love is an outlet of something much deeper and more personal than mere physical pleasure. It's obvious to me now that one is a lot harder to come by than the other." Three weeks later Vivienne wrote similarly, "The fact is that she [Laurel] really needs constant love, and this creates both physical and mental problems for her. She has known all along that I disapproved of fucking anyone but the one you love."

When Laurel appeared to be pregnant in August 1973, what troubled Vivienne most, Laurel felt, was the implied promiscuity. The baby's father would have been someone that Laurel cared little about, whereas Vivienne had liked and approved of a boy with whom Laurel had been involved for over a year (see page 83). Not wanting to acknowledge her concern, Laurel feigned a nonchalant attitude. But to Vivienne this made it appear that Laurel was taking the situation too lightly. Vivienne, both Anne and Paulette thought, seemed to feel betrayed by Laurel. "Laurel has promised me this hasn't happened," Vivienne told her mother; "but," said Paulette, "it had."

There were hints of pleasure and no lack of curiosity about relations between the sexes on Vivienne's part. But these were inevitably overtaken by her conflicts. When she was just twleve she enjoyed a dance at a yacht club in Maine. Her father and several older boys danced with her and she wrote happily in the diary, "Well, it was exciting for me, because I've never, never been asked by a boy before in my life! They swung me around and we laughed and got all hot and happy. (If they just knew I had only just turned twelve!)" We can recall the delight Vivienne took in her friends' spying on the couple "making it" in the red car parked on "Lover's Lane" (see pages 60–61). But such instances were rare. For the most part she sought to fend off the pressures of sexuality within and without as best she could by delaying her active participation.

An almost exclusive emphasis on the spiritual aspects of sexual relations and romantic love is found in both sexes during adolescence. Spiritualization is one way to defend against or postpone the anxieties associated with erotic sexuality. Traditionally this form of sublimation tends to persist longer and to be sustained with greater intensity in girls than in boys. But this may be changing with the greater sexual freedom encouraged now for girls in our society and the increased pressures upon them to engage in early sexual activity, including sexual intercourse.

Vivienne's search for the ideal in herself and others found its most characteristic expression in relation to sex and romantic love. Her idealization reflected her personal values regarding intimacy and love while at the same time defending her against the onslaught of physical sexuality. "I'll probably keep my ideals for the time being. Of course, I don't have, and never have had, any hang-ups about marriage. I just require a deep and caring love," she wrote John May shortly after she turned fourteen. Her ideals sometimes proved insufficient to discourage certain boys, especially the older ones. At these times she might resort to her trick of pretending to faint or have a fit, which generally was effective in discouraging any further advances.

Vivienne's father said — and who could possibly disagree with him — that "it would have been good if she had some sort of a soulmate, someone near her age, or a boy perhaps — a boy who was a little older in actual years, and who was on her general plane in the way of looking. . . ." But the intensity of Vivienne's idealization prevented her from having ordinary friendships with boys near her age. Her love for John May filled her imagination, but he had left and was unattainable. "I wish you were here," Vivienne wrote to him a few weeks before her death. "Just to be here. You were my very best friend; you still are (not that you've got any competition)."

The American culture in which Vivienne was growing up was particularly destructive to a child of her sensitivities and vulnerabilities, and contributed ultimately to her death. We may begin with her experience of sexuality. On August 9, a week before her fourteenth birthday, Vivienne wrote to John May, ". . . One guy tried to rape me five days ago, and I haven't seen him since. Mommy and Daddy would have a fit if they knew, but I didn't find it as traumatic as everybody seems to make it. The fact is that this particular fellow had already had a few six packs too many. It had nothing to do with me." Two weeks later she wrote, "Three times, three people in the last 2½ weeks, have tried to fuck me. Twice I was good and stoned and once I was bored stiff. But each time, I just thought to myself — God! Is this all there is? Not only is there no true love, no giving — but this is all as routine as taking your vitamins in the morning. I don't see how you get Saturday night 'fun' out of it."

What does this mean? Laurel and Anne told us of the boys in Maine and the ones at home ("really raunchy," Anne called them, on the basis of Vivienne's description) who tried to make violent sexual passes at Vivienne. Curious, following Laurel's lead, Vivienne went along. But where Laurel, sixteen, could handle herself fairly well, Vivienne could only frighten the boys away by her trick of pretending to drop dead, which, Anne said, "would freak these guys out." Anne doubted that Vivienne "felt anything sexual." What strikes me about these experiences is how unprotected Vivienne was. She was distant from her mother, and could not confide in her father, despite her wish to be close to him. Further, she was drawn precociously by her need to follow Laurel into situations she could not handle. But there is something more, which, I believe, can only be understood in terms of some sort of breakdown in the social structure.

Late teenage boys seem to take for granted that they can attack a fourteen-year-old girl sexually without risk to themselves, and Vivienne herself, in the matter-of-fact tone she assumed in her letters, appears also to have accepted that she was fair game for such conduct. She seems to have absorbed a compliance with the mores of the society around her. Her parents, "moralistic" as Laurel felt at least her mother to be, sensed no mandate to guide their daughters in sexual matters. On the contrary, they felt enjoined from knowing or from intervening. Society offered no protection. Instead, it seemed to encourage sexual behavior that undermined what self-protective defenses Vivienne was forming, and forced premature sexualization of her adolescent relationships. She was denied the delay in dealing with sexuality that she needed. Peter Barglow, a psychoanalyst, and Margaret Schaeffer, a psychologist, who are experts in the field of female adolescent development, have written that for the young girl, "postponing sexual activities until she and her male partners have acquired greater capabilities for adult intimacy and responsibility is probably a positive protective step rather than a negative retarding one." [18] Vivienne made clear in her letters — her denial ("I didn't find it as traumatic as everybody seems to make it") notwithstanding — that the undermining of her idealization of sexual relationships deepened her disillusionment and contributed significantly to her depression. Adolescents, especially those whose way of holding off sexual anxieties is to idealize intimate relationships, need to allow themselves some sexual experimentation at their own pace. A society that sets no limits, that, on the contrary, encourages sexual assaults upon early teenage girls, is *itself* destructive to their development. It is likely that Vivienne's experience in this respect is not unique or even unusual.

Sexuality is not the only part of her life in which Vivienne was unprotected by her culture. Her parents spoke of Vivienne's sensitivity to the social and political problems and injustices around her. As she took on the burdens of her family, she assumed, in addition, the problems of the world. It was primarily through television that Vivienne was assaulted with the failures of adults in the larger world. David Loomis understood well what this exposure meant for his children and especially for Vivienne. "She somehow took too much of a load psychologically onto herself," he said. "They are seeing a lot of tragedies and injustice in the world through television. Not just the immediate people of the family and friends have troubles in the world, but you see very graphically singly and in groups ... through television, people in all parts of the world, all the tragedies that go on and injustices. And these just bothered her so much, and she somehow bore this as a great sorrow and burden and grief, and yet what could she do about it? She was just caught in this overwhelming — ... Where we value such involvement and sensitivity ... say in the war in Indochina — the news from the war there. She didn't get numbed by it, and turn it off, maybe as many people got to accept the casualty figures. No, she was the other extreme. ... She kept taking this seemingly upon herself."

One may argue that it was not the constant bombardment with the news of Indochina or Watergate, or the conditions of our prisons, or the treatment of the American Indians that injured Vivienne, but her precocious sensitivity, her excessive idealism, her abnormal idealization, which made her vulnerable to the impact of these social problems. This is true, but it is also not enough. The emergence of the ego ideal has become more complex for girls as a result of the expanded options open to them. As traditional conceptions of valuable goals for a girl are challenged, the examples of current adult conduct outside of the family become more important. If in addition to the inevitable disillusionments within the family, early adolescents are daily confronted with overpowering instances of corruption in the social and political world, the task of forming stable and enduring ideals may be greatly complicated. The image, for example, of a president leading the moral corruption of a nation, hammered home daily through the mass media, seems to be destructive to the development of personality itself in early adolescents.

It is likely that a child with Vivienne's unusual sensitivities needs to be protected from too much real evidence of the moral depredations and pain of the larger world, from assaults of the mass media, especially television. It is probably true that adult human beings do not behave worse individually and collectively than they ever did. But there is little protection now of the young, few barriers against the steady stream of viciousness that pours into every living room day and night. The horrors of reality have overtaken the evils that once were more limited to the imagination among the young. By 1962 Peter Blos could write, "Themes which once were dominant in diaries — the instinctual conflicts and their accompanying depressive moods, colloquially known as *Weltschmerz*, a melancholic cosmic grief — have given way to different themes, which may best be summarized as a diffuse anxiousness about life . . . the political naiveté and provincialism of bygone days have been dramatically replaced by an awareness by most adolescents of world-wide sociopolitical conflicts." [19] I doubt that the diaries, poetry, school compositions and letters of even the most sensitive thirteen- and fourteen-year-old children in an earlier time would have been filled with such matters as the editorials of the *Manchester Union Leader*, the stock market, Senate hearings, prison horrors and the pollution of the earth. This is the gift of the mass media to our young. If the media are helping to educate some, they are perhaps also contributing to the destruction of others.

Vivienne's Death

For Vivienne life had come to contain too much agony. Death became in the end a welcome relief from pain. From Vivienne's standpoint the choice of suicide was no more irrational than a similar decision of a patient with terminal cancer or of a prisoner facing certain execution. The future appeared similarly to offer no hope. "There are times / When I have nothing / To look forward to / In life / At all," she wrote, a year before her death. All of the unfortunate circumstances that preceded Vivienne's death — the moves of school and home and the several losses she had recently experienced — are secondary to this central fact. Vivienne chose to die in order to relieve unbearable pain. As Henry A. Murray has written, "For what is suicide in most instances but an action to interrupt or put an end to intolerable affects?" [20]

Why was Vivienne's pain so intense? Why could she foresee no likelihood of its relief? How could death become a solution for her?

"I am of no use to anyone," Vivienne concluded at the time when she first seriously began to contemplate ending her life. Nothing in the eight months remaining to her relieved for long this hateful self-judgment. It became in the end intolerable. What is it that is so unbearably painful in this conflict about self-worth? Freud asked a similar question about mourning in 1915, that is, why the "detachment of libido from its objects should be such a painful process." [21] In the need to experience oneself as having value we seem to have arrived at a kind of human bedrock, analogous in the emotional sphere to vital tissue injury in the physical. It seems to be essential to human life to experience oneself as having some kind of worth. Conversely, to consider oneself to be of no value, to be "nothing," as Vivienne saw herself, and to feel helpless to bring about any change, is unutterably painful.

Vivienne's inability to foresee that her depression would ever lift, that she had any hope of ultimately obtaining relief from her pain, is an important element in her decision to kill herself. Although her depression was not always present, Vivienne's poetry and journal entries convey a conviction of permanence. Losses cannot be replaced. Broken dreams are shattered forever. Anne Tucker expressed to us clearly the lack of perspective about life and death that she had shared with Vivienne, and that was to some extent characteristic of their immaturity. "I think when you are fourteen life isn't so precious," she said. "It wasn't as if we had some kind of perspective on what the rest of our lives would be like. Everything was very much *then* and very much involved with what we were dealing with then... now I think about things — what I am going to do after I get out of school. We weren't thinking about that at all. We were thinking about right now — not next year in high school even."

Lacking perspective about the permanence of her distress, Vivienne was able to consider suicide as a solution by distorting the nature of death and by actively working to overcome her fear of it. Rob has suggested that his coming "up to the edge" of suicide was known to Vivienne and may have influenced her choice. As she experimented with fainting and strangulation, and rehearsed her suicide, Vivienne became, as it were, on familiar terms with death, and able to experience "what my dead face will look like immediately after the killing." She became familiar with the sensations of partial strangulation, which seemed to lose its horror for her. Ultimately death itself became a kind of idealized object with which Vivienne actively sought union. Toward the end she told Anne that she expected death would be peaceful, like a cloud, so easy. "Death is going to be a beautiful thing," she wrote across the downstairs bathroom wall where she had once rehearsed her strangulation. David Loomis felt Vivienne had developed a fascination with death, while Paulette had the impression Vivienne thought "there would be some great revelation" upon her death and "everything would resolve at that point." It seems clear that Vivienne had successfully transformed death from something dreaded and bleak to an idealized realm. Rather than a feared or awesome prospect, death became a solution for Vivienne by virtue of being itself distorted into the perfect and self-completing object she had always been seeking.

As she had written in her book report on Elie Wiesel's *Accident* in December 1972, Vivienne had "often thought of death as a retreat" for herself. Her poetry became more filled thereafter with death images and in April, after John's departure, she began to think seriously about ending her life. The first serious "experiment" with killing herself occurred in July. After this events seemed to conspire with Vivienne's self-destructive intent to bring about her suicide. Once, however, Vivienne came to view her situation as hopeless, and discovered that she could use death as a solution, she seems to have been the prime mover behind these events. The pill-taking gesture in Maine, although perhaps a signal of distress, served by virtue of its transparently manipulative aspect more as a decoy, diverting her family from the seriousness of her intentions. It was Vivienne who selected as her friend at Cambridge School of Weston a classmate whose sister had recently killed herself, and she became identified with this girl and her sister. In the counseling sessions Vivienne expressed her distress and the wish to be known and understood, but chose not to reveal her thoughts about suicide and death.

Vivienne did share with Laurel and Anne her thoughts about death and much information about her suicidal experimentation and plans. But she disqualified them as potential saviors by elevating their secrecy to the level of a sacred trust. Vivienne's secret was very "precious," Anne said. To have told anyone would have been a betrayal. "I could never have said anything to anybody," she said. "It was just very sacred."

The shift to Cambridge School of Weston, Vivienne's separation from Laurel (who went to a different school), the family's imminent move, her father's professional dislocation and the many problems of her mother that were brought to Vivienne were all what might be called "aggravating factors." Rob summed up the coalescence of several disturbing elements: "In her own life there was such a great erosion, and in the life of all those around her and in the political life of the nation." The disruption in the family and in her external life corresponds to Vivienne's inner turmoil. Paulette spoke and wrote of the turmoil in the home in preparation for the move, of packed cartons and rolled-up rugs. Vivienne near the end wrote in her poems of "tension on the verge of snapping," of the splintering of the day and the scattering of dried flowers, of "inner riot." The organization of the family and the household is represented in the self and helps to bind its structure. When fragmentation in the family takes place, or is experienced, a corresponding sense of coming apart or splintering may take place in the ego or the self in vulnerable family members, especially children or young adolescents.

Although suicide was planned out carefully, Vivienne remained in conflict about her decision and fearful of it to the end. She and Anne "hold each other up from day to day," Vivienne wrote on December 11. But her last supports seem to have pulled away in the final days. Anne was still grieving over her sister and the ten-year-old retarded girl she had cared for, and could not bear to hear Vivienne talk seriously of suicide. She was about to leave on a Christmas vacation with her family. Vivienne's parents were caught up in the move and less available emotionally. On the night of the suicide they were at a neighborhood good-bye party. Laurel too was defending herself from the stress of the move and from Vivienne's pain by shutting everything out. She was "lost" in music while Vivienne was carrying out the suicidal act and was only "dimly aware" of Vivienne. The suicide itself, Vivienne's "finalizing chord," was a climax following the "crescendo" of which she wrote at the end. The black stallion threw her. She could no longer stay astride. But the stage had been methodically set by powerful psychological determinants on Vivienne's part that made her vulnerable to collaborating factors and circumstances in the world around her.

Ever since Freud wrote that suicide represents a turning against the self of murderous impulses originally directed toward an object in the outside world, the assumption of conscious and unconscious hostility toward another person has been given a great deal of weight in psychoanalytic and related theories of suicide. Otto Fenichel in his classic *Psychoanalytic Theory of Neurosis* even wrote, "The thesis that nobody kills himself who had not intended to kill somebody else is proved by the depressive suicide." [22]

This theory does not apply well to Vivienne's case. In the circumstances of her death there seems to be manifest evidence that the act was directed toward her mother. Vivienne used rope that her mother had given her and it was in Paulette's silversmithing studio that she hanged herself. She complained of being unequal to the burdens of her mother's confidences and called her with some irony and apparent anger "My Little Princess." The journal and poems of her last three years seem to be an ambivalent bequest of this child to her parents. Laurel felt that Vivienne was angry in the last weeks and certainly experienced her "leaving" as a hostile act, and Vivienne wrote in a poem that "rage" had become "half of life." There was a strong taboo in the family against direct expressions of hostility toward others, although Vivienne could be quite combative in discussions. Vivienne herself left two statements that relate specifically to how she linked suicide with feelings toward her family. To John May in her last letter she referred to a note she had left by her bed following one of her suicide experiments which said "*something* like 'I didn't want you to think that it was because of you when it was only me all the time.'" In the journal entry of July 9, 1973, following her first serious suicide attempt, she had written, "With regard to my family: I realize that my death will upset their lives; some more than others. However, I am sure now that I would upset their lives more by staying on here and living this life. Surely they do not deserve it. They will never realize what I have spared them. I will go with the knowledge. I hope it is a kindness to everybody. I have loved them very much."

Yet there really is not much in all of this to support the interpretation of Vivienne's suicide as *primarily* an act of hostility directed toward her mother or anyone else. The request for rope and the choice of her mother's studio permit other interpretations, such as the wish to be merged with her mother in the final moment. The evidence suggests that her love for her family seems to have acted as a constraint against suicide. But Vivienne was not a patient, and the poems and diary materials do not provide a complete view of her specific unconscious motivation. It is possible that there were hostile wishes behind her act that are not apparent in the available material and from which her conscious mind was defended. Our data support more strongly, however, a view of Vivienne's suicide as motivated by the wish to relieve overwhelming pain in the context of loss and of the shattering of the psychological structures that sustain self-esteem. Its execution (after her first serious attempt Vivienne referred to her suicide as "the killing") was made possible finally by a quasi-delusional transformation of death itself into an embracing and peaceful self-object. Edward Bibring, interestingly, regards "the aggressive impulses against the self," the self-hate seen in depression, as secondary to the breakdown of self-esteem. The rage is the outgrowth of the feelings of powerlessness of the ego.[23]

Any suicide is experienced as a reproach by those who have been close to the person who has chosen to die. Survivors are left with feelings of guilt that derive from the inevitable conviction that one has failed to do something that could have prevented the outcome. Suicide thus becomes by its very nature an indictment of a family and its society. But the painful experience of those who are left behind must not be assumed to reveal the specific psychological motives and determinants of the act.

Finally, there is a religious element in Vivienne's life and death, difficult to place and to document. There is little evidence that she held formal religious beliefs. Her religion was private, even mystical, her mother thought. The family's Unitarianism was flexible and nondoctrinal. Her father wished Vivienne would attend church, which she did sometimes, but he did not insist upon it. She found the "God seminar" taught by John May "sort of boring," he said, but argued fervently for religious tolerance in the essay she wrote for it. There was a strong spiritual quality in Vivienne, a reverence for the sacred. She wrote in a poem once of leaving "My inner soul unhidden as a high price to pay for believing." She participated in the popular musical *Godspell*, and enjoyed especially singing in the Melrose Episcopal Church choir.

The raw essentials of Vivienne's life course leading up to her suicide might be summarized in this way: early injury to the developing self was followed by unusual sensitivity to loss, persistent and profound doubt about self-worth, and severe disturbance in ego-ideal development. In early adolescence a major loss of an idealized person, perceived as essential for the value of the self, together with a multitude of other disappointments in the people and the world around her, activated underlying conflicts in relation to self-worth, which were experienced as intolerably painful. After a period of experimentation, during which the reality of death was transformed into an imagined state of beauty and solace, the final act of suicide emerged as a chosen solution to an overwhelming dilemma.

Vivienne and the Problem of Adolescent Suicide

It would be valuable to know whether these observations about Vivienne's life and death represent a pattern that could be found in many or even a majority of other early adolescents who choose to die. There is an extensive literature by now on teenage suicide but very little in the way of study in depth of particular adolescents who have killed themselves. The French writer George Bernanos, in his short novel *Mouchette*, has told the story of a fourteen-year-old French girl who drowned herself.[24]

Mouchette is the child of an impoverished village family. Beaten at home by her father, and ridiculed and humiliated at school, she emerges from early childhood as an unusually sensitive fourteen-year-old; "often a gesture or a single word could upset her terribly." Confined during a storm with a drunken poacher, she feels an emerging tenderness and maternal protectiveness toward him. But in a drunken fit of lust he rapes her "at the height of her humble love." Mouchette experiences a depth of shame and humiliation she cannot articulate. She turns to her mother for advice and affection, but the woman is dying and in pain and also burdened with a new baby. The mother dies before Mouchette can tell her of her experience. Her father insults her and is incapable of understanding. She then experiences further stigmatization and deepening shame in the village, and her self-hate grows. An old woman who tells her, "I understand the dead," and talks to them, helps Mouchette to consider death as a possibility for herself and to overcome her fears of it. A "deep secret impulse toward death" grows in Mouchette. A "desire for revenge" against the man who abandoned her "might have taken the place of hope" and have saved her. But instead her hopelessness and "inexorable sense of futility" grow. "Once they have been induced to despair," Bernanos concludes, "the defences of the simple are irretrievably breached and their ignorance knows of no escape save suicide...." In the end Mouchette chooses to leave a world she experiences as indifferent to her pain. *Mouchette* is a dramatic tale, a fiction. Yet many of the girl's qualities — her unusual sensitivity, the linking of the loss of love with the destruction of her self-worth, the growing sense of futility and isolation, the difficulty of finding someone who will understand, and, finally, the grasping of death as a solution — remind one of Vivienne.

Diaries seem to be a promising source for understanding the inner life of adolescents who are struggling with suicide. At a time when most teenagers find it difficult to confide in anyone, a diary can be a kind of uncritical and totally accepting object to which the deepest and most private thoughts and feelings may be communicated. Keeping a diary is assumed to be a common activity among adolescents, especially girls, whether or not they are especially troubled. It would be interesting to know how often the decision to start a diary is a sign of distress or reflects the struggle of a young adolescent to ward off depression. Addressed often in the second person, a diary becomes an object for the adolescent midway between a real person and a fantasy. Diaries seem uniquely well suited for helping adolescents who are struggling with loss, and for setting down the feelings experienced in connection with disappointments and griefs. Anaïs Nin began her famous diary when she was eleven, after her father had abandoned the family. It was started originally as a letter to him, intended to keep him informed of her "wanderings far from him," and hopefully to bring him back. "Dear Diary," she wrote at thirteen, "pity me, but listen to me." "At the core of my work," she wrote later, "was a journal written for the father I lost, loved and wanted to keep." "Everybody wants to deprive me of the journal," she complained, even as a young adult, "which is the only steadfast friend I have, the only one which makes my life bearable." [25]

One sixteen-year-old girl, Andrea, who had been struggling with a depression that resulted in a moderately serious suicide attempt, observed about her diary, "I started the whole journal because I was depressed." She sought to write her "way out of it" by exploring in its pages "where I was going, who I really was" and also what there might be about her that was "unique." Another suicidal adolescent girl who was receiving intensive psychotherapeutic treatment told her doctor simply, "The diary is my best friend."

Although two years older than Vivienne was at the time of her death, Andrea revealed in her journal many of the same struggles. In the weeks before her ingestion of pills (from which she survived relatively uneventfully) Andrea's journal was filled with her doubts about her self-worth. She took inventories of her qualities and capabilities and concluded she was not smart or attractive enough or sufficiently special. She longed to be an artist ("I wanted my art to be very powerful, moving to make people feel, hate, love..."), but she did not believe she was creative enough to achieve her aim. As with Vivienne, obesity was a problem ("I feel I am too fat"), and when depressed Andrea would gorge herself with "junk" or "shit" foods. In the diary Andrea expressed her longing for intimacy and for someone her own age with whom she could communicate. Like Vivienne, Andrea seemed injured by the demands upon her for precocious sexuality, that she "just fuck people." Also, like Vivienne, Andrea longed for perfection in relationships and was repeatedly disappointed that nothing and no one was ever "fully complete, sincere, honest. Not even me." No one was ever up to her exalted "standards." "It pains me," she wrote, "it pains my heart to see people so ridiculous, pitiful, non-feeling and non-thinking." Andrea, like Vivienne, seemed exposed too rawly to the impact of social problems and they caused her much suffering. "Do you know we are wrecking Nature! We are killing it, like killing off the whales. Society doesn't care or think. Assholes, just assholes." "I am vulnerable in society," Andrea wrote in her journal. "If you are nice you get hurt," like "The Good Person [sic] of Setzuan." Andrea, like Vivienne, revealed what she called her "unrealistic love" of an older man ("My only real love"), and wrote of the pain his loss had given her. This loss seemed closely linked to the fall in her self-esteem. The worst pain, she said after the suicide attempt, was "not liking myself."

Andrea contemplated suicide as a relief of "life, torture, pain" that had become intolerable. She looked on the act of suicide as a way of taking responsibility for her plight, and, like Vivienne, learned to imagine death as a positive state. "I will have bliss," she wrote, "I will have nothing." Andrea struggled with her hostility and feared the pain her death would inflict on others — "I hate receiving pain, and giving it to someone else is just as painful for me." Perhaps this conflict, her ability to imagine and to identify with the pain of others who loved her, acted as a restraining force in Andrea's case and contributed to the failure of her attempt to kill herself.

In 1977 over two thousand boys and girls between the ages of ten and nineteen deliberately ended their lives in the United States. In 1977, suicide passed homicide to become the second leading cause of death in the fifteen-to-nineteen age group. In the quarter century between 1952 and 1977 the suicide rate in this group tripled. Although the rate remains low in the ten-to-fourteen period, this too is rising about as fast. Unsuccessful suicide attempts are many times more common among adolescent girls than boys, while boys outnumber girls three or four to one in completed suicides. When a boy attempts suicide he is, therefore, many times as likely to mean to do it all the way, a phenomenon yet to be adequately explained. If one considers that many homicides are the result of provocation on the part of the victim, and that large numbers of accidents — the leading cause of death between fifteen and nineteen — are the result of self-destructive motivation and behavior, the proportions of the problem loom still larger. Furthermore, there is no comparable increase in the suicide rate in the older age groups, except in the group aged twenty-five to twenty-nine. For example, in the decade between 1968 and 1977 the suicide rate increased 135 percent in the fifteen-to-twenty-four age group. During the same period the overall suicide rate in the United States was up 34 percent, with most of this increase accounted for by those under thirty. Even if we allow that a greater contemporary willingness to report suicide affects these statistics, suicide among the youth of this country has, in any event, become a formidable problem, a tragedy of increasing magnitude that requires study and understanding. Calvin J. Frederick, chief of emergency mental health and disaster assistance at the National Institute of Mental Health, referred to the recent rate of suicide among adolescents as "a monumental increase." [26]

Emile Durkheim, who is widely regarded as the pioneer of suicide studies, wrote in 1897 in his famous *Suicide*, "Suicidal behavior is a combination of psycho-instinctual impulse and social precipitation." [27] But researchers on the subject of suicide have struggled with difficulty over the problem of this "combination." Clearly, statistics such as those cited above make one wonder what has changed in society, what "factors" external to the young people who have died may be cited to account for such a dramatic increase in the rate of adolescent suicide. There is a growing literature in suicide studies that addresses this question.

But research of this nature will not shed light on the question of why particular adolescents decide to kill themselves, while others choose, no matter how difficult they find their existence, to continue to live. The late Gregory Zilboorg, in his 1937 paper "Considerations on Suicide with Particular Reference to That of the Young," called for "a proper study of the individuals lost behind the statistical figures." [28] But in an essay only a decade ago the psychoanalyst Paul Friedman, who edited the Vienna Psychoanalytic Society's 1910 discussion of suicide, still asked whether "we better understand the individual who is driven to suicide than we did at the first symposium," and stated that "research in depth of the individual in his . . . development must still be our primary concern." [29] Yet studies that concentrate on the psychological dimension, the factors within the individual that led to the suicide or suicide attempt, will not generally tell us much about the part played by social forces in the outcome.

Vivienne was not a "typical" child of her age — if there is such a person. She was, for example, unusually articulate and rather precocious in many of her insights. Perhaps Vivienne's case, however, when viewed both in its social context and in its psychological depths, encompasses a sufficient number of variables that should be considered in an individual suicide to suggest a model of how external and internal forces articulate or augment one another. It is clear that the roots of Vivienne's suicide, and probably that of other adolescents, are both social *and* psychological, and that the truest understanding of the act will come from knowledge of how these forces relate to one another. Vivienne's life and death provide an especially rich opportunity to observe the complex interplay of social and psychological determinants.

An Architectural Model of Adolescent Suicide

Max Warren, who recently reviewed the subject of suicide from a psychoanalytic perspective, wrote that "the structural point of view offers the best framework for the understanding of suicidal behavior, albeit even if it is incomplete." [30] What Warren is asking for is a view of suicide that takes into account the total organization of the personality, its component agencies, such as the ego, the ego ideal and the superego, together with the development of the individual and his or her relationships with other people. A structural approach would also be incomplete if it focused too narrowly on personality organization and neglected the ongoing part played by the family, the community and the society more broadly.

I would propose what might be called an *architectural model*, which would regard suicide as the final act in an extensive set of determining forces — biological, psychological, interpersonal, familial and social — that build, not necessarily in a regularly sequential or orderly fashion, toward the final outcome.

A reconstruction of the elements in a given case, the survey of its particular architecture, might begin with genetic or constitutional factors, the role, for example, of a family history of depression or suicide, or specific evidence of biological susceptibilities in infancy. Or one might start by examining the family or community into which the child was born. Following this one would trace the disturbances of development at each period of childhood that might contribute to the vulnerability to suicide. We would look especially for evidence from the child herself that events, experiences or influences hypothesized to be of significance have actually had a discernible impact on her emotional and personality development. We would look to see how the organization of personality seemed to be crystallizing during the adolescent period, paying particular attention to the coalescence of elements that we have come to understand tend to be associated with depression. As Francine Klagsbrun concluded in her extensive study of young people who had attempted suicide or thought seriously about it, "The majority of people who commit suicide do so as a result of ... devastating depression." [31] At each stage of development one would consider the reverberation of family life and relationships, of the experiences in the neighborhood, school, community and larger society (particularly as transmitted through television) upon the child's developing view of herself and her world.

Finally, one would look at the circumstances and, if possible, the thinking of the adolescent in the weeks and months leading up to the suicide, taking note especially of "what made the difference," or what were the "last straws," what made it possible to overcome the barriers to suicide. The same model could be extended to adult cases as well.

Once we understand better the critical determinants of suicide it may not be necessary to look so systematically at the totality of the child's life. But for the present such an extensive biographical or architectural approach may be helpful in identifying the elements that seem to be of central importance.

Studies of suicide by clinicians have suffered from a lack of the kinds of data that would permit the systematic examination I have in mind. Reports of suicides, or of cases in which suicidal impulses figured prominently, are rare on the part of psychoanalysts. The successful suicide of a patient, or even a serious suicide attempt, is an extraordinarily painful experience for a therapist and understandably difficult to write about. Also, a plan to commit suicide, even in an individual who has contemplated ending his life for a long time, or has made earlier suicide attempts, is a deeply private matter that, very often, will not be reviewed with a psychotherapist. The documentation that Vivienne's journal and other writings provide enable us to learn a great deal about her inner life and private thoughts. There is a tradition in psychoanalysis of learning from autobiographical documents, the Schreber case, in which Freud worked out many of the mechanisms of paranoia, being the best-known example. But a written document is not the same as the words of a live individual, who can give us the opportunity to ask the questions we must in order to understand. On the other hand, when it comes to suicide, especially in young adolescents, one is dealing with an often secretive area, and has no choice but to take advantage of whatever information may come along.

Studies of suicide among adolescents by Robert Gould, Charles Shaw, James Toolan, Albert Schrut, Kurt Glaser, Elizabeth McAnarney and others stress the frequency of divorce, abandonment, broken homes and parental rejection or loss in the families of suicidal adolescents. Statistically, these factors do seem to be important. Vivienne, however, came from an intact home without parental separation, divorce or physical loss. John May, who spent much time with the Loomises, including a few days in which he lived with the family, found them to be loving and warm, showing real concern for one another. Our impression has not been different. David and Paulette were, however, too burdened with their own problems and emotional pain to fully comprehend what Vivienne was experiencing. On her part, Vivienne was so held back and depressed that she may have been unable to recognize their caring.

How is it that the statistics regarding the relationship between family instability and suicide seem to have little application in Vivienne's case? Vivienne might be an exception. The dynamics of suicide might be different among middle-class families, or Vivienne could represent a "type" of suicidal adolescent in which these elements of family disruption do not apply. Perhaps the essential psychological preconditions, although more likely to occur in situations of family disruption or loss, may develop within an individual child with or without actual loss of a parent or other serious breakdown in the structure of the family itself.

There have been several efforts in recent years to relate the increasing incidence of suicide among the young to Durkheim's notion of anomie, or the breakdown of norms and values in the society. Durkheim's fundamental hypothesis, which has proved very difficult to test, was that suicide varied directly with the degree of disintegration of domestic, political and religious life in the society. A recent study has indeed shown a correlation between the increase in the suicide rate in the fifteen-to-twenty-four age group and personal expressions of anomie, such as a view of the social order as unpredictable, of community leaders as detached, or of personal relationships as no longer supportive or meaningful. Another psychologist studying family status and anomie has also suggested that adolescent suicide may be an extreme reaction to family alienation or anomie. It is difficult, however, to demonstrate how anomie, or the social alienation of a particular child or adolescent, played a part in the development of his or her inclination toward suicide.

In Vivienne's case it can be demonstrated that the family's alienation from *its* community, especially her father's rejection by his church in Melrose, affected her powerfully. Furthermore, the environmental problems and political corruption she observed in American society, what she called "a dog-eat-dog world," caused in Vivienne a profound moral revulsion, and had a destructive impact on her early adolescent development that contributed to her suicide. She was unusually vulnerable to these experiences.

Vulnerability is a notion that is gaining increasing currency in psychology and psychiatry. It refers to those hereditary, constitutional, developmental and environmental factors that make a child at risk. But vulnerable to or at risk for what? It we say "for suicide," there is little research available to identify relevant aspects of such hypothesized vulnerability. Evidence is emerging that a vulnerability to suicide may be genetically transmitted. Frank Schulsinger, Seymour S. Kety and co-workers in their study of nonfamily adoptions have found that there were 12 suicides among 269 biological relatives of 57 adoptees who committed suicide. Among the group of 148 adoptive relatives — that is, nonbiological relations — which included the parents who raised the children that committed suicide, there were no suicides.[32] In an as yet unpublished study Kety and his co-workers have found 15 times the expected concentration of suicide among the biological relatives of adoptees studied because of their depressive illness.[33] These findings suggest there is a population that is hereditarily at greater risk for suicide but that psychological and environmental factors determine the suicidal outcome in specific cases. There is no known history of suicide among Vivienne's relatives.

The question of constitutional vulnerability to suicide is more complex. Ever since Paul Bergman and Sybille Escalona demonstrated in 1949 that there were some children who could be shown to be unusually sensitive in early childhood to colors, lights, sounds and other sensory experience, there has been the hope that such sensitivities might be correlated with later childhood or adult psychopathology, especially psychoses. Studies of temperament or characteristic modes of functioning of infants — their activity level, quality of mood, rhythmicity, intensity of reaction, distractibility and attention span — by such researchers as Stella Chess, Alexander Thomas, Michael Rutter and James Cameron have shown that these characteristics have some but by no means consistent correlation with later behavior patterns. All investigators stress the fundamental importance of the interaction of infantile risk factors with the personality of the parents and other environmental determinants. Cameron has used the metaphor of a geological fault, the constitutional vulnerability or risk representing a kind of biological strain point or weak area that may predispose to later disturbance if a certain set of environmental conditions or interactions of constitution and environment take place.

In the case of suicidal behavior among children and adolescents, the evidence is no more than suggestive. Charles Shaw and Ruth Schelkun found that children who seem most susceptible to suicidal behavior tend to be hypersensitive, rather suggestible, and tolerate frustration poorly. These authors are explicit in stating that they are referring to children who made suicide attempts that were unsuccessful, considering the "successful" suicide to be "beyond study." [34]

As James Toolan, one of the leading investigators in the field of adolescent depression and suicide, has noted, "The vast majority of youngsters who threaten or attempt suicide are depressed to a significant degree." [35] Certainly the kind of deliberate suicide we are considering in Vivienne's case grows out of a deep depression. This raises the question of whether it is useful to consider the source of vulnerability to depression in adolescence. Very little work has been done on the question of a constitutional predisposition to childhood or adolescent depression. No consistent biochemical abnormality has been noted in depressed children or adolescents, much less one that would distinguish a group of *infants* predisposed to depression. Some babies have been noted to respond to frustration with an excessive tendency toward inhibition, withdrawal or unresponsiveness, while others seem to become anxious.[36] But it is difficult to separate constitutional predisposition from infant responses that are already reflective of disturbances in the mother-child relationship. Furthermore, there are few or no data that correlate observations of infantile response patterns to later childhood or adolescent depression. The problem is further compounded by the consideration that not all adolescents who are prone to depression are inclined to become suicidal. Thus, if it is difficult to identify in infancy a constitutional predisposition to adolescent depression, it would seem at this stage of our knowledge virtually hopeless to try to identify the elements of a constitutional predisposition to *suicide* in adolescence.

A study by Stephen Applebaum and Philip Holzman published in 1962 of Rorschach test responses of hospitalized psychiatric patients is of special interest. They found that adult patients who had made suicide attempts, or who subsequently committed suicide, gave color-shading responses on the Rorschach cards, that is, went beyond the givens to search out nuances of perception or feeling, far more frequently than did several control groups. The authors suggest that the suicide-prone individuals have "a keener eye for what is there...an articulating, discovering and fluctuating activity." They propose that "in adequately functioning people of superior intelligence, such sensitivity and capacity for differentiated responsiveness may be available for adaptive uses, for example, in discriminations between ideas, deep inquiry into the uniqueness of objects, empathy for the nuances of another's experience, and the appreciation of art." Applebaum and Holzman speculate that "the price of such near-sighted clarity" can be "a short-sighted perspective of one's historical continuity" and, therefore, a proneness to suicide due to "a feeling that one has run out of alternatives." These individuals would be "better served," the authors suggest, "if they were buffered by the refuge of greater generality, less involvement, and an increased ability to 'let it go at that.' " [37] Although the average ages of Applebaum and Holzman's suicidal experimental groups were thirty-two and thirty-three, these descriptions bear an uncanny resemblance to Vivienne's personality. Applebaum and Holzman do not speculate as to whether the color-shading response of suicide-prone individuals is an inborn proclivity or the result of developmental experience.

Vivienne's parents noted from early infancy a special sensitivity, a tendency to place few demands and to withdraw when disappointed or hurt. Later, according to Laurel, Vivienne developed a temper and "could be impossible when angry." But in reconstructing her life it is virtually impossible to distinguish a constitutional or biological element from the parents', and especially her mother's, relationship to her, or to view her responses to them as anything other than the product of relationships that were already established. For whatever reason, from an early age — perhaps already in the second year — Vivienne seemed to be structuring her own experience, to be an active agent in eliciting particular responses from her mother. She may, for example, have encouraged her own rejection by tuning Paulette out.

What might be looked for in the first years of life that could have some bearing on the vulnerability to later suicide? Some children exhibit head banging and other forms of aggression directed against the self, but no one seems ever to have attempted to link such behavior with later suicidal tendencies. Reginald Lourie, a prominent child psychiatrist, has suggested that an infant's tendency to react to separations from its mother by turning away from her may be a pre-stage, the earliest expression of the child's struggle to master the reality of separation, loss and, ultimately, of death itself. But such temporary rejection of the parent by the child after separations is commonplace and does not distinguish one child from another. Possibly if the mother reacted to such turning away by her own withdrawal, a pattern of mutual rejection might develop that could have ominous significance for the child's future relationships and patterns of adaptation. But the specific relevance of such patterns of withdrawal in childhood to a later tendency to suicide remains to be shown. Similarly, Calista Leonard has suggested the hypothesis that inflexible patterns of responding to conflicts over dependence and autonomy established during the second and third years of life might predispose to suicide. Such inflexibility leads to an individual's finding himself later without inner resources for dealing with conflicts involving violence, hostility, loss and fear of death. Although the validity of Leonard's theory has not been established, there is a need for hypotheses about early ego organization that might make some children vulnerable to suicide, which can be tested through long-term follow-up studies.

Early childhood loss of important love objects has often been invoked as a predisposing element in the histories of suicidal adolescents. But how do such losses bear on the vulnerability to suicide? How does the experience of earlier loss and death become translated by the adolescent into a predisposition to suicide as a solution to his own personal life dilemmas? Herbert Hendin in his studies of suicide among college students has identified a group of young people among whom suicide or death has become a way of life. He has found a pattern of "dead relationships" among these youths, dating back to early childhood, a "bond of emotional death" with family members and others who are simultaneously both needed and hated.[38] Suicide paradoxically becomes a return to a dead life. There remains, however, the need to explain how such a process might become established in a particular child.

The early childhood vulnerability to suicide seems to derive, above all, from processes of identification. But, identification with whom or with what? Zilboorg has written with a tone of authority, "... Only those individuals who appear to have identified themselves with a *dead* person and in whom the process of identification took place during childhood or adolescence, at a time when the incorporated person was actually dead, are most probably the truly suicidal individuals. Thus, when a boy or a girl loses a father, brother, mother or sister at the time when he or she is at the height of their oedipus complex [age three to five] or transition to puberty, there is, in case of a neurotic reaction in later life, a true danger of suicide." [39]

But how does this work? If we grant that the identification in early childhood with the lost or dead person has something to do with a later tendency to suicide, there is still much to explain. Why identify with the "death" aspect of the person who is gone? Why not identify with other qualities, such as his values or ideals, as other children often do? What bearing do the actual personal attributes of the lost person, or the qualities of the child's relationship with him or her, have on the risk of suicide? What connection is there between such identifications and the so-called epidemics of suicide in which young people follow the example of another adolescent or adult who has committed suicide? [40] And what a vast amount of uncertainty is betrayed in the phrase "in case of a neurotic reaction in later life."

James Toolan suggests that the suicidal child takes upon himself certain "bad" qualities of the parents rather than "acknowledge" their "badness." In assuming the "burden of evil he attempts to absolve the parents." Joseph Teicher and Jerry Jacobs quote from a letter of a seventeen-year-old black adolescent to his father before his second suicide attempt. "Daddy you just don't know just how much I bare [sic]," the boy wrote.[41] This bearing of burdens, especially of others', was certainly important in Vivienne's suicide.

Vivienne's strong reaction at two upon her parents' return from Europe was more than a turning away. She seemed not to recognize her mother and would have nothing to do with her for several days. Removing herself, as a means of reacting to painful separations and human encounters, was already established by age two and followed the experience of her infancy in which great emotional distance developed between Vivienne and her mother.

Vivienne's sensitivity took a form in her fifth year that seems to have a greater specific bearing on the question of her vulnerability to suicide. We saw her unusually strong identification with the pain of loss that each of her parents experienced at the time of the death of their fathers. We have seen how the memory of the loss of her mother's father, who "used to tell me that . . . *dreams* were for pursuing," haunted her a few weeks before her death and became the embodiment of all that was lost and past. Her parents felt that there was a direct continuity from the early childhood sensitivity to her parents' pain to the tendency she demonstrated throughout her life to carry the burdens of each family member's troubles and anguish as if they were her own, and to respond so strongly to the inhumanity she learned about in the world outside the family. From an early age Vivienne identified readily with the pain of the world's victims. She was afflicted by her own empathy, a quality we generally prize. During the elementary-school years Vivienne became herself a victim of the cruelty of others, but by this time her vulnerability to victimization was already well established.

The most specific dimension of Vivienne's vulnerability to

suicide resided in the organization of her personality. At the core of this vulnerability was the problem of self-regard, the inability to experience herself or her world as having enough value to make living tolerable. On pages 146–152 we saw how her emerging ego ideal, the agency of personality carrying the principal responsibility for regulating self-esteem, became a rigid taskmaster, insisting upon the most exalted standards of human conduct and intimacy. As Anaïs Nin wrote in her diary, "[the idealized] image is always a great strain to live up to. Some consider the loss of it a cause for suicide." [42]

I have suggested that the particularly uncompromising quality of Vivienne's ego ideal was the outgrowth of injury to her self-development in infancy and early childhood, and that thus the task of finding serviceable ideals, with which all adolescents must struggle, was loaded with the additional burden of repairing her injured self or of redeeming the crippled sense of her own worth. André Haim, whose book *Adolescent Suicide* considers many of these questions, has also noted the "peculiarities" in the organization of the ego ideal in adolescents who are prone to suicide. "One is dealing with an archaic megalomaniacal ego ideal," he wrote, with a "demand for the absolute" and "absence or inadequacy of reshaping when put to the test of reality." From this perspective, loss of a love object such as John May, who has been idealized in order to fulfill redemptive or reparative purposes, becomes a precipitant of suicide by virtue of the essential function the person serves in maintaining the very structure of the self. Without the love object the self becomes nothing, of no value, and the experience of being shattered, or of going insane, of which Vivienne wrote, takes place. This is surely one of the "dangerous ways of loving" of which Freud warned, in which the ego is overwhelmed by the object.[43]

The ego ideal links the inner self with society, with the outside world. Like the ego itself, upon whose functions of perception, judgment and evaluation it must rely, the ego ideal mediates between the internal and the external worlds. It is built on the one hand upon the internalization of parental values and expectations, while at the same time it looks to society to provide objects and examples with which to structure more realistic aims and goals, as the idealized and omnipotent images of the parents of the early years become modified during later childhood and early adolescence. But the selection of models or examples is powerfully determined by the residual needs of childhood and the early organization of the ego ideal. In Vivienne's case we have seen how deeply affected the structure of her ego ideal was by early injury to the self and by the example of parents, especially her mother, who sought to fulfill through this child, from whom she felt estranged, her own longings for perfection.

Thus Vivienne, instead of beginning that process of compromise and modification of ego-ideal expectations, which even normally causes much disappointment and pain in adolescence, was trapped between the perfection of her expectations and the disillusionment of reality. The discovery of the brutality of the outside world, whether of the cruder side of sexuality or of the reprehensible behavior of trusted leaders, caused shattering disappointment. Television denied her whatever distance a child of another generation might have experienced. Land, air and water pollution, abuse of prisoners and Indians, White House plumbers and Vietnam flooded her consciousness. "The Stock Exchange, / Neon signs, / Traffic jams, / Indo China, / Another exam and the Watergate. / New train tables, / Inflation, highway repairs, / Nixon, / His dog 'Checkers,' / Your new bugged home," as Vivienne wrote in one of her poems, became an integral part of the "whole death syndrome."

Paul Friedman is the only writer on suicide among the young to link its increased frequency to sexual and other forms of permissiveness. "I wish it were possible," he wrote, "to take a close look at the permissive, overindulgent parents and school authorities so characteristic in this present era of the so-called sexual revolution. By their failure to institute and maintain appropriate and essential control, they have added tremendous confusion to the natural oscillations of adolescence and greatly complicated the process of maturation which, unfortunately, enhances not the libido but the aggressive instinct." [44] A conservative tone, perhaps, but one that Vivienne shared. She stated bluntly on the subject of sex and morals, "I don't think that I can follow the nation's trend." She followed its trend in suicide instead.

I would not claim to find the cause of suicide in Vivienne's case, or in that of any other adolescent, in the outside world. As I have tried to show, the vulnerability to suicide lay primarily in Vivienne's constitutional predisposition, her early childhood injuries, the patterns of her identifications and the structure of her personality, especially the ego ideal. I would argue that the failure to protect the young from bombardment with the shattering failures of our generation — perhaps not in themselves worse than those of other periods of history — results in lowering the threshold of vulnerability, or of increasing the number of actual victims among the potentially vulnerable. Most difficult of all to assess among these "failures" of the adult generation is the context of imminent nuclear annihilation in which all children now grow up. A recent study by the Task Force on the Psychosocial Impact of Nuclear Advances of the American Psychiatric Association suggests that adolescents are more deeply troubled by this threat and what it means to them than has heretofore been realized.

There remains a central nagging question. Most depressed adolescents, even if they think about suicide, are not drawn to it as strongly as Vivienne was. Why suicide? Why not another way of responding to her depression? Other ways might presumably include, for example, taking drugs or alcohol, which might relieve her pain or call her plight to someone's attention. Or what about sexual experimentation, an avenue well known among adolescents seeking love, excitement or relief of pain. One can only answer that for Vivienne, and perhaps for many like her, this was not her way. Endowed or burdened with strong and quite rigid superego prohibitions, Vivienne could not permit herself the kind of impulsive or "acting-out" behaviors that often relieve adolescents temporarily of their emotional pain however much such actions compound their real problems. The one "public" suicide gesture she allowed herself, the pill taking in Maine, failed ultimately in its communicative purposes. Although this act was more impulsive than was Vivienne's usual style, it was, nevertheless, a highly calculated and carefully aimed performance. It is a paradox of Vivienne's short life, and part of her tragedy, that impulsive or short-term solutions were not available to her. Qualities of depth, personal determination and deliberateness characterized Vivienne as they must many other adolescents who decide to end their lives.

A similar argument might apply to why Vivienne did not succumb to schizophrenia or to another form of psychotic illness that removes the self from unbearable emotional pain by sacrificing contact with reality. Again one can only reply that it was not in the nature of Vivienne's ego organization. Although she felt at times as if she were going insane, Vivienne remained firmly in touch with reality to the end, except in her estimate of the future, and, perhaps, in her view of the nature of death. It was, in fact, her inability to obtain any sort of distance from the presence of her pain that made suicide ultimately, for Vivienne, like Mouchette, the only solution. Suicide was for her an alternative to psychosis or severe mental illness.

A great deal has been written about the failure of suicidal adolescents to *communicate* their intentions or their distress. If Vivienne was in any way representative of seriously suicidal adolescents, this generalization must be carefully qualified. Vivienne's state of mind and suicidal preoccupations were clearly communicated to three people, John May, Laurel and Anne Tucker. What she gave them was much more than "signals." John May, for his own reasons, could not bring himself to acknowledge how serious was Vivienne's depression and did not or could not act to intervene. In the case of Anne Tucker and Laurel, Vivienne had successfully persuaded each of them of the sacredness of her trust and made them swear not to tell anyone else. Perhaps at some level Vivienne hoped they would tell someone, but for practical purposes Laurel and Anne were drawn into the service of her suicide plan. In the case of her parents, Vivienne had come to assume their burden as her own, much as in the cases of parent-child role reversal described by Douglas Kreider and Jerome Motto among suicidal adolescents, and could not share her pain with them directly. Paulette reached out to allow Vivienne to make her feelings known but Vivienne feared her mother "wouldn't like it if you did know me." The question of communication, then, needs to be refined. One must ask, communication of what, to whom, when and in what form, and must also consider the receptivity of and options available to the persons receiving the messages. Francine Klagsbrun found, for example, in her survey of 113 high-school and college students, that 49 percent answered "yes" to the question "Do you think suicide among young people is ever justified?" [45] It is interesting to speculate whether this represents a shift in attitude toward suicide among American youth, or suggests that suicide as a response to depression is becoming not only free of sin but socially acceptable among adolescents. In any event, it does suggest that a communication from one adolescent to another about suicidal intentions will not necessarily be conveyed to a responsible adult if the suicidal youth is able to persuade the other boy or girl of the rationality of his plans or purposes.

But the central and, in some ways, most frightening aspect of adolescent suicide is its increasing attractiveness as a *solution* to personal situations viewed as being without hope or without the possibility of change. If Camus is correct that "killing yourself amounts to ... confessing that life is too much for you," then more and more adolescents are making that confession.

A good deal has been written about the distorted time sense of adolescents, who, it is said, cannot anticipate that the future might change. But suicide has also increased in frequency in adults under thirty, whose time sense is, presumably, fully developed. The relative immaturity of the intellectual functions of the adolescent with respect to time is probably less important as a factor in adolescent suicide than the subjective experience of a particular child that his or her *personal* future is without hope. This certainly was so in Vivienne's case.

Suicide has long been viewed, by individuals who choose this course, as a solution to a personal reality experienced as emotionally intolerable. The French sociologist Jean Baechler, in his comprehensive study, *Suicides,* has demonstrated in hundreds of individual instances how "an act of suicide is always undertaken in order to resolve a situation in a certain way." [46] This was clearly true in Vivienne's case. The *totality* of her existence, the losses she had experienced, and the burdens and shortcomings of those close to her, for whom she felt a precocious and exaggerated responsibility, became more than she could handle, more than she could bear. Suicide became for Vivienne an alternative arena of mastery.

Many persons who have contemplated suicide have written of this element of seeking mastery, of the struggle to take charge of one's existential dilemma through suicide. The French dramatist Antonin Artaud wrote, "By suicide I introduce my design in nature, I shall for the first time give things the shape of my will ... now I choose the direction of my thought and the direction of my faculties, my tendencies, my reality." [47] Jo Roman, the artist who suffered from cancer and sought to end her life "on my own terms" in June 1979, was trying to take active charge of her death through her suicide, rather than to succumb passively and helplessly to the advances of a debilitating malignancy. Jo Roman's cancer was not extensive at the time of her suicide, and she chose to exchange a number of months and possibly years of life for the right to take charge and to stage dramatically the time, place and form of her death.

Teicher and Jacobs have shown that among many adolescents suicide has become "the only alternative" after a period of longstanding and "escalating" personal problems. In Vivienne's case suicide began to take shape as a solution to her dilemma of loss and pain at least eight months before her death. She experimented with it, sought to free herself of its terror and, ultimately, planned her end with great deliberateness. Far from being impulsive, her final act was well crafted and methodically executed. One cannot help wondering whether it was their sense of the affirmative quality of Vivienne's suicidal activity that prevented Anne and Laurel from intervening.

The "romanticizing" of suicide, of which Richard Van Del has written recently, may be part of the process through which suicide becomes a possible solution for an adolescent. Death becomes transformed — delusionally if one does not believe in an afterlife or a heaven — from the cold cessation of life into a kind of imagined paradise. Maurice Friedman and several colleagues, who studied in psychoanalytic treatment adolescents who had attempted suicide or self-mutilation, found that death had the meaning of profound peace and freedom from disturbing sexual and aggressive drives and fantasies.[48] In Vivienne's idealized view, death became a time of everlasting peace, something beautiful where all would be revealed and resolved. For this child, who longed so intensely for intimacy and perfect understanding, dying seems to have had the same meaning it had for Mann's Dr. Faustus, that of a return to the mother of earliest childhood. Born in the throes of an experiment in natural birth, of a mother seeking perfection, Vivienne ended her life in her mother's workshop after experiments that made of her death a near perfect creation of her own.

Discussions of suicide often begin with a classification of types of cases. The classification may be based on behavior (impulsive versus planned); choice of method (hanging, overdose, firearms); psychodynamics (psychological mechanisms or motives); psychiatric diagnosis (depression, character disorder, schizophrenia); or upon the meaning of the act itself. Ake Mattsson and his co-workers divided into six categories seventy-five children and adolescents who were referred for suicidal behavior to a psychiatric clinic. The groupings, based on predominant behavioral manifestations, were: (1) those with grief after loss of a love object; (2) markedly self-depreciating patients; (3) those "crying for help" beyond the immediate family; (4) revengeful, angry teenagers; (5) psychotic adolescents; and (6) those playing "the suicidal game," flirting with death.[49] James Toolan divided children and adolescents who attempted suicide into five categories based on dynamics, or "causes," of the attempt: (1) anger at another internalized as guilt or depression; (2) attempts to manipulate another to gain love and affection or to punish; (3) a signal of distress; (4) a reaction to feelings of inner disintegration; (5) a desire to join a dead relative.[50] Jean Baechler has identified eleven "types of suicide," which he calls "typically distinct situations where suicidal action could be considered as an adequate solution." Baechler's classification is intended to distinguish "the general meaning or sense of the act." [51] The eleven types are flight, grief, punishment, vengeance, crime, blackmail, appeal, sacrifice, transfiguration, ordeal, and game.

Such classifications, while convenient for those working with the problem of adolescent suicide from special clinical or theoretical perspectives, inevitably restrict our view of the subject.

Classifications like Mattsson's, which stress behaviors or motives, may impose a limited focus upon a particular case, while excluding other categories that may also apply. Similarly, more than one of Toolan's psychodynamic mechanisms may be found in any given case. Classifications like Baechler's, which seek to interpret specific meanings behind suicidal action, may also exclude other "meaning or sense" of equally great relevance to a full understanding of the problem. Vivienne's suicide, for example, when examined comprehensively, contains in some degree virtually all of Baechler's eleven types. Classifications phrased in the language of clinical psychopathology exclude important elements in the suicide decision, such as active self-assertion, the desire for mastery, or the accurate current assessment of one's dilemma, all of which reflect strengths in the personality. The risk, then, of adhering to such classifications is that their use may prematurely foreclose the search for understanding, may cause one to focus upon certain observations while data of equal importance are overlooked.

At the core of the problem of suicide is inevitably the question of the value of one's life and one's self. All of the categories of adolescent suicide in which there is a serious possibility of death seem to involve the experience of worthlessness, inability to anticipate a better future or a sense of helplessness to change it in a positive direction. The biographical, or architectural, approach I have used in presenting Vivienne's life and death grows out of our wish to examine the social framework, psychological development and human relationships of one child in order to try to understand how this experience of worthlessness came about.

Jerry Jacobs, in his study of fifty adolescents who attempted suicide, places an emphasis similar to ours upon the detailed study of actual cases, including psychiatric interviews of the child and family members. Jacobs calls his approach "morphological" and has undertaken "the chronological ordering of social-structural events found in the detailed accounts of the suicide's biography as he related them." [52] Jacobs stresses the events leading up to the suicide attempt following a long-standing history of troubles, and "the escalation of problems" beyond the adolescent's ability to cope with them. He also points to the crucial importance of the adolescent's progressive isolation from meaningful social relationships. Jacobs places less emphasis than I do upon the internal organization of personality, the psychological predisposition that makes the self-regard of the adolescent vulnerable to the problems that crowd in upon him during "the final stage" and that come to be viewed as "insurmountable."

The model suggested by Vivienne's case, and others we have reviewed, for approaching the biography of a potential adolescent suicide contains a number of dimensions that might be summarized as follows:

1. The setting, including the family's place in its community, the network of relationships established in the neighborhood or town, and the family's relative "fit" within or adaptation to the values of the surrounding population

2. The personalities of the parents or principal caretakers, siblings and other important relatives, their expectations, experience and, above all, their perceptions about child rearing and interactions with a particular child

3. Genetic and constitutional factors or special sensitivities that might make certain children vulnerable to injuries of self-development and, ultimately, to depression or suicide

4. The predisposing developmental experience, especially those injuries to the self that grow out of disturbances in the early parent-child relationships and that ultimately affect the internal regulation of self-esteem

5. The experiences of loss in childhood, the responses of the child (and other family members) to such losses and the identification with the lost person, or with the parents' experiences of grief or loss

6. The emerging childhood personality organization, especially the idealized expectations for oneself and others, which make the child vulnerable to injury to self-regard when later disappointments or losses occur; the crystallization of an inflexible and unrealistic ego-ideal structure in adolescence

7. The emergence of an actual tendency in the child or adolescent to respond to losses, rebuffs and other hurts, real or imagined, with indications of fall in self-esteem, significant depression, withdrawal, or other changes of behavior or mood

8. The adolescent's ongoing experience of success and failure, especially in human relationships, of friendship and alienation, of love and loss, especially during the last months before the suicide or suicide attempt

9. Evidences of undue preoccupation with death, and its emergence for the adolescent as a possible solution to his or her dilemma in the face of intolerable feelings of worthlessness and emotional pain

10. Lack of protection within the family, community or nation from social and political problems that bring about deepening disappointment or disillusionment with the outside world, especially as experienced through television; exposure to sexual assault, expectations for performance or experiences of exploitation that lead to further self-devaluation

11. The increased acceptability of the solution of suicide among adolescents in a society that cannot protect them in a world with a doubtful future

12. Last events — losses, separations, disappointments, disrupted relationships, family moves, preceding suicide threats and attempts, unsuccessful treatment efforts, missed communications (including appeals for help), failures to heed signals or to intervene — all of which may allow the balance finally to shift toward suicide

Further in-depth studies of other adolescent suicides will tell if this framework or model for approaching a particular case has any general usefulness.

Clues, Signals, Communications and Prevention in Adolescent Suicide

The suicide of a child or adolescent is a tragedy of virtually unspeakable dimensions, especially for those who loved the young person and must live with the hurt that remains. Any contribution to the prevention of such a loss, and the pain that must follow, seems worth the attempt, especially as the frequency of successful suicide in adolescence seems to be increasing. Furthermore, although clear-cut data regarding the effectiveness of therapeutic intervention are lacking, it is the impression of many clinicians that most adolescent suicides can be prevented if the problem is identified and effective treatment initiated.[53] This is not surprising. Personality structures, such as those described in this book, are not yet rigidly fixed in adolescence, however powerfully they may influence the individual's attitudes and emotional state at the time that he or she is considering suicide. In addition, the actual decision to kill oneself, although it may have been incubating for many months or even years, is, nevertheless, strongly affected by the situation that immediately precedes the suicidal act. Powerful affects, especially intense feelings of sadness, hopelessness and rage, can impair acutely judgments about the future and the permanence of circumstances that seem, at the time, to be utterly without the possibility of change for the better. The balance of the decision between life and death may be delicate, swinging precariously, as in Vivienne's case, from one side to the other before the point of no return is reached. It is for this reason, as B. D. Garfinkel and H. Golombek point out, that the suicide may appear to be precipitated by an apparently trivial event.

Adolescents seem not to make dangerous suicide attempts without giving clues to someone in advance, however subtle or indirect the indication may be. The suicidal adolescent is very likely to have experienced, as Mattsson and his colleagues, Mary

Susan Miller and others have noted, a serious breakdown in the ability to communicate troubled emotions to parents, including depressive or suicidal feelings. It is especially important, therefore, that other family members, friends, teachers, physicians, clergymen, or anyone who comes in contact with the adolescent, be alert to possible signals or indications of depression or suicide risk. Such signals, in addition to specific suicide threats or talk, include evidence of increased moodiness or that the child seems "down," sad or uncommunicative; voicing of feelings of personal worthlessness or discouragement; withdrawal from activities; turning to a diary instead of people; friendlessness or breaking off of friendships; school failure or lowered school performance; school compositions revealing a preoccupation with death or other depressive content; increased drug and alcohol consumption; acting-out, antisocial or impulsive behavior; hypochondriacal bodily complaints; and increased philosophical preoccupation with death and dying.

The social relationships and academic challenges of junior high school and high school provide an arena in which many of the conflicts over self-image and self-worth are played out. It is for this reason that so many suicides seem to follow disappointments and failures in the school setting. Jacobs has written that, of the large group he has seen of adolescents who have attempted suicide, one-third had recently dropped out of school, most for reasons other than specific academic failure. Academic failure, or the fear of it, certainly can, however, precipitate suicide. A recent epidemic of suicides among school-age West German students has been attributed to a punishing system of preselection for higher education and the threat that the student will have no future if he does not do well. The problem in West Germany, where the suicide rate for those under eighteen is 50 percent higher than in the United States, seems to be compounded by punishments or harsh reproaches from parents when poor report cards are brought home.[54] In such epidemics it is likely that the identification of students with those who have killed themselves recently is a contributing element in the clustering of suicides in a single school or community.

What might have been considered clues in Vivienne's case? It is easy in retrospect to identify many alarming indicators and messages, even though her diary's contents were unknown. Paulette and David Loomis knew that Vivienne was depressed through much of the fall following her suicide gesture in Maine and made efforts to reach out to her. Paulette told us that she "didn't want to bring up suicide a lot" and felt at a loss about what to do. The counseling was an effort on the parents' part to achieve greater communication within the family, even though it failed in its purpose. Vivienne never communicated the depths of her despair to her parents or gave any direct indication to them of her more serious flirtations with death.

In the case of Laurel, Anne Tucker and John May the problem is not one of clues or signals but of their response to definite communications of serious suicidal intention, including the history of major previous attempts. Laurel and Anne were drawn into Vivienne's view of reality and accepted at some level her right to end her life in this way. Each felt she would be breaking a trust that at the time seemed of a higher priority than intervening to prevent further suicide attempts. In "a very basic way" Anne never really believed Vivienne would actually kill herself. John May had also been given clear communications about Vivienne's depression, suicide attempts and continuing suicidal thinking. It is still not entirely clear to John why he did not intervene more actively. He cared about Vivienne, but was in over his head. He was in California during the period in which Vivienne was writing to him about suicide and believed that the problem was being handled at home and that the family was receiving counseling. He too could not bring himself to believe that the situation was as ominous as it was. Perhaps he had too much confidence that his supportive words would make the difference. Now, he says, he handles suicidal adolescents differently, holding back from allowing them to share too much about their problems, urging them instead to seek psychiatric treatment.

The responses of the Loomis family, of Anne Tucker and of John May to Vivienne's communications demonstrate the need for educational programs that can help to alert parents, peers, teachers and other school personnel to the indicators of depression and potential suicide in children and adolescents. Terror of the possibility of suicide, of thinking the unthinkable, may immobilize those who do care but are afraid to validate their own suspicions or are unsure about what to do with the information, once they have it, that a child or adolescent is at risk. Educational programs provided by informed mental-health professionals can help to lower the threshold of suspicion, describe the clues to suicide, overcome the reluctance to face the fact of jeopardy, and increase the confidence of peers and caring adults in inquiring matter-of-factly about the young person's state of mind. The objective of such educational programs is not to turn friends, parents or teachers into psychotherapists. It is, rather, to enable them to identify suicidal children and adolescents, to feel able to talk supportively with them, and to be unafraid to act decisively in urging young people at risk for suicide and their parents to seek psychiatric or other competent professional help. Calvin Frederick of the National Institute of Mental Health believes the juvenile suicide rate can be reduced through training nonprofessionals such as teachers, counselors and teenagers themselves to recognize suicide danger signals.

The school is a vital resource in any adolescent suicide prevention program. Teachers have an unparalleled opportunity to observe and interact with teenagers and it is to teachers, directly and indirectly, that they will often turn, as in Vivienne's case, when they are having emotional difficulties. Mary Susan Miller, a former schoolteacher herself, has written, "School personnel are as vital to suicide prevention as parents — and not just counselors and teachers: the secretary from whom the student feels no demands; the nurse who listens; the janitor who lets him help. A wise guidance department will arrange meetings to alert the school staff to the symptoms of suicide and to their role in its prevention." The school, Miller says, needs to function as a "translator" for the meaning of adolescent behavior that may portend a serious problem. Jerry Jacobs, a psychologist, thinking along similar lines, has recommended "programs designed to increase and extend interaction between troubled students and their peers and teachers" in order to "increase the potential for establishing meaningful interactions" and reduce "the potential for suicide." [55]

We are suggesting here a vital role for teachers and schools, but one that is limited to the identification of an adolescent at risk as a step in suicide prevention. When they reach out, teachers may go a long way toward "treating the hurt" in the child or adolescent to whom they find themselves responding with empathy and love. But it is important for them to realize the limits of what they can undertake and know when to ask for professional help. The adolescent who is vulnerable to suicide will most likely have suffered deep personal wounds and loss in earlier, failed, love relationships. A teacher who allows himself to mean too much to the adolescent runs the risk of repeating the experience of hurt and loss when the separation or disappointment inevitably takes place.

"Sometimes the family can't help," Vivienne wrote, at least not to relieve the hurt and loneliness that can lead to suicide. It is for this reason that most students of the subject of adolescent suicide recommend psychotherapy by a competent psychiatrist or other mental-health professional once the suicide risk is identified. Because the problems are most likely long-standing, such treatment should continue for months and even years, and the therapist needs to be available to the young person even after the immediate risk is no longer thought to be present. A close working relationship with key family members is important for the therapist. Family members *can* help, by learning more about the problem, facing up to it, and increasing their availability to the child or sibling. Often hospitalization is necessary when the suicide risk is considered severe and a secure working relationship with a therapist has not been established. Adolescents resent psychiatric hospitalization, often bitterly, and the experience, especially in badly run units, can in itself be traumatic and a blow to self-esteem. In such instances the indications for hospitalization or the risks of suicide have to be weighed against the major disruption of the adolescent's life that institutionalization causes. It is best to lean on the safe side, but not to allow the hospitalization to continue longer than is necessary.

Even though the drive toward death may be strong indeed in an adolescent, prompt treatment is often effective, for there are usually equally powerful doubts about suicide, forces holding on to life in the young person. The balance is often so delicate that a harsh word or a supportive talk with a friend, teacher or therapist may make, at least for a brief time, the difference between death and life.

A fourteen-year-old boy who had just been helped to grieve for the loss of his father, who had died a few months before, said that the main problem he had encountered previously in talking of his feelings was the sense that each person with whom he tried to broach the subject found it too difficult to bear. He had decided, therefore, to keep his pain to himself, which ultimately became intolerable. The principal goal of the psychotherapist is to restore the positive self-regard of the suicidal adolescent, to help the young person regain a sense of his or her own worth. The process is begun by listening, by hearing and experiencing the pain associated with countless rebuffs, disappointments and frustrations. Psychotherapy is a kind of emotional holding. The therapist of the depressed or suicidal individual provides a safe way of loving, one upon which the young person can rely. Once such a trusting, caring relationship is established, the task of therapy is to repair the injury to self-regard that dominates the clinical picture. Ideally a skillful therapist should seek to achieve structural change in the personality of the suicidal adolescent. This means going beyond immediate support, or the ventilation of troubled emotions, to bring about a change in the balance of forces within the self. Structural changes would include a softening of the self-critical voice of judgment, the development of more realistic aims and ideals that are realizable within the world that exists, and, ultimately, the repair of self-regard through remembering, and the healing of early injury that can come when the remembering takes place in a new and caring relationship that validates and acknowledges the essential worth of the individual.

Treatment with the goal of achieving such far-reaching results requires a therapist of great skill, sensitivity and timing. In many instances such an individual may not be available. But one should not forget that in an adolescent the forces of life are on our side, and that the balance may often be helped to shift from dying to living with an intervention less intense than that described above. As Vivienne wrote in her discussion of Elie Wiesel's *Accident*, "Like the man in the book, this stage in my life is one of depression. But unlike the man in the book, I have learned to live for Spring. . . . The difference," she continued, "between life and death (by will) is having the strength to stand up (again?)." It is not always so great a task to help a suicidal youth to stand up again and live for spring. But first we must find out.

HOLLY HICKLER

A Teacher's Viewpoint

IN SEPTEMBER 1973, forty new ninth-graders arrived at the Cambridge School campus in Weston, Massachusetts. They came in car pools and trains, in the school van, or trudged across the fields if they lived nearby. For the most part, they were day students and they joined the 260 other boarding and day students of the upper classes. They arrived hopeful and skeptical, each one dragging the successes and failures of previous experience.

In Vivienne's case, hindsight provides a warning. "I am drawn to death," she wrote in her application, and we are not comforted to read her final words in that essay, "Death will befall me; I will not befall death."

Although the Cambridge School Admissions Office had not seen her extension of this thought in a book report, eighth-grade teachers at Cambridge Friends School had undoubtedly read her sentence, "I have often thought of death as a retreat." Did her teachers regard this as the poetic musing of an introspective child? Was the word "retreat" a part of her lexicon as a minister's daughter? Was she telling them that life had exhausted her?

When young people are tragically lost, adults retrace their

steps like bedeviled detectives: Was it here the clue was dropped? Was this the point that could have changed the outcome? Was that meant to gain attention? A false lead? The simple revelation of danger? Parents walk these paths and stare at the evidence, accusing themselves at every turn. Teachers sort through their responsibilities. Before the fact of Vivienne's death, they stand sickened, confused, looking for explanations.

Vivienne's despair was well hidden when she came to the Cambridge School in 1973. She appeared to be a pleasant and cooperative new student in the nine weeks she attended classes. Her admissions essay remained in the Admissions Office, along with her high marks from Cambridge Friends and her superior test scores. The only mature person who knew of her depression was three thousand miles away. Vivienne had arrived with a fatal inward loss. No adult on the campus was aware of it.

Cambridge School of Weston, unlike Cambridge Friends, is set in a suburban wooded countryside. The roads approaching the campus are punctuated with old stone walls, occasional farms and horse-show fields. Even in its early days Cambridge School expressed an interest in "a concern for the individual as a whole being, for initiative and self-determination and for close association between student and teacher," as its handbook still states. In 1931 Headmaster John French, a friend of John Dewey, stated the school's philosophy: "The school exists for the child — not the child for the school. The only enduring discipline is self-discipline; and the only education worth its name is self-education. Every school experience should contribute to steady growth in capacity for self-direction and in attitudes and habits of social responsibility." Certainly the Cambridge School was founded on principles that could support sensitive children like Vivienne.

Always considered a progressive school, Cambridge, one of the first coeducational boarding schools in the United States, has characteristically offered a rich program of arts that shares the dignity of academic courses and the chance to work warmly and personally with teachers. Students serve in the school's administration and on its board of trustees.

When Vivienne arrived, the school was in its first year of the module system, a modern attempt to extend John French's principles of forty years before. The module system divides the year into seven miniterms and allows for total immersion into one or two subjects at a time. It provides an opportunity to add experiential learning to intellectual study (John Dewey's theory that "to do is to learn"). The faculty in 1973 was both excited and challenged by these changes.

Into this galvanized atmosphere Vivienne came, a new ninth-grader. It is never easy to start any school where unknown teachers and students await you. Personal safety is in question: Will I fit in? Will anyone like me? Can I be successful?

At the first school assembly old students greet each other while ninth-graders look on, newcomers, not sure where the library or science building is. Vivienne Loomis and Anne Tucker, both new students, didn't know each other and had no presentiment of how the future would bring them together. They attended that first assembly and were sorted into classes. By chance, they ended up in the same English course.

No matter how often they have done it, teachers too face their beginning classes with a mixture of hope and apprehension. Faces blend, discussions start slowly. It takes days before a new group becomes distinct and individual. Vivienne's teacher didn't know her well, and when I was invited to teach a one-day creative writing assignment in Anne and Vivienne's class the group was unfamiliar to me.

I remember entering that room full of ninth-graders. Fall had sharpened, and the big glass windows looked out on skeletal trees and slightly shimmering air. I came armed with ideas about writing portraits. What do we notice about people who make an impression on us? How do they characteristically stand, talk? What analogies do they suggest? What is a typical setting for them? What qualities strike us that make them memorable? I plunged into my project, often asking for discussion and debate. I remember that we played an analogy game using people we knew in common: What color would express that person best? What animal? What time of day, kind of food? At the end of class I gave a portrait assignment for that night.

I returned to my regular classes and thought little about my one day with the ninth grade. Then the portrait assignment came back to me a few days later. Vivienne's poem "To My Father" was in that pile of papers. I was immediately struck by the poetic imagery and feeling.

I saw Vivienne that day on my way to lunch. She was walking with Anne. They seemed engrossed, and from a distance, I imagined their heads were actually touching. I stopped and told Vivienne how much I liked her poem. She seemed to bend under my praise. Her head was lowered and she gazed, not at my face, but somewhere near my knees. I had copied out some poetic portraits for her (one by E. E. Cummings, I remember) and I searched in my book bag and found them. As I handed her the pages, I suggested she submit her poem to the school's literary magazine. She mentioned this in a letter to John May.

At a school assembly after Christmas I learned Vivienne was dead. The headmaster read from her work, "The Most Important Thing to Me Is a Friend" and "I Am the Youngest in My Family." We all sat in numbed silence. I looked at Laurel and Anne. They were sitting together. Laurel stared at the floor, Anne gazed out the high gym window. Then I thought of the father in Vivienne's poem. I had not met him, or any of the Loomis family except for Laurel. I next tried to imagine Vivienne's mother. Stricken for her sake, I tried to picture Vivienne again. All that came back to me was the bowed head and the lowered gaze.

In the days after that assembly, I was haunted by questions: What could we have done for Vivienne when she was here walking on our campus? What could I have done? What can schools and teachers do? What could we learn from her despair that would help other young people?

I called Mrs. Loomis and asked if I might see more of Vivienne's writing. She generously gave me all the work she could find. Gradually Vivienne's story unfolded. It was a tragic one, but in my experience, not at all unique.

In my teaching career, I have taught all ages. I have known children far more apparently injured than Vivienne, even abused. I have known adolescents with fewer successes and, to an observer, deeper feelings of worthlessness who nevertheless survived. Even Vivienne's preoccupation with death, had I known of it, would not have shocked me. The idea of personal death has impact at any age, but for adolescents it has particular force. Many young people struggle to incorporate their new awareness and even toy with death as a possible means of controlling their own destinies. In last year's creative writing class, Jenny wrote in a tenth-grade journal: "I try to think and nothing is clear.... It's as though a black curtain is separating me from my brain.... I want to live, yet I want to die.... Why?" [1]

Few teachers take such sentiments lightly, but in Jenny's case I had other reference points to help me understand her depression. I knew that Jenny had unfinished business at home and that she was frightened and ambivalent about her friendships in a new school. I had seen her perform in a play, had watched her at lunch in the cafeteria, and had observed her animation in the halls and with classmates on the quad. Nonetheless, I spoke seriously with Jenny and helped her arrange some counseling. In this way, teachers have the advantage over parents. They can keep touch with the life-styles of their students in far more detail and for many more hours of the day than any other adult. "The role and influence the teacher assumes is secondary only to that of the parents in the adolescent's life," Norman Kiell comments in *The Universal Experience of Adolescence.*[2]

In some ways, the role of the teacher is more than "secondary" for young people. Teenagers tend to shut the door on parents. Their struggle for privacy and independence often rules out intimate conversations at home. "How was your day?" we ask our high-school son or daughter. The reply is brief and neutral: "Fine." Sometimes a teacher knows better and can help when parents are barred from confidences.

Unlike Jenny, Vivienne did not send signals to any Cambridge School adult and her pain was not visible. Her deepest injuries had occurred before we knew her and she had become clever about concealing them. But suppose we had known her longer than her brief nine weeks with us? Suppose we had seen some of her most dramatic writing? It takes an experienced eye to detect the difference between fatal despair and sensitive introspection. Adolescents are often dramatic in their writing. To an adult, young people sometimes seem to lack an emotional thermostat, so heated and volatile are their responses. They can be anguished at one moment, restored and vivacious the next. One must know a great deal about them to judge how serious their struggles are.

But all adolescents do struggle in one way or another. It is the hallmark of their development. Erik Erikson observed that the identity-seeking in the adolescent involves change, conflict and anxiety. As a teacher and a parent, I have seen this striving at first hand. I have watched my own five children and other young people I teach. They arrive from childhood into altering bodies and changed expectations. They face developmental tasks that take many years to accomplish but are posed with special urgency in high school: separating from family, making new and deeper friendships; integrating sexuality; visualizing a personal future and maintaining self-esteem without unusual reward or punishment. In the course of facing these struggles, young people often describe in their writing disappointments, depressions, loneliness, feelings of loss and helplessness, worries about desertion, friends, school. It is not unusual for them to ponder death.

By the time I see them in classes, many of the young people I know have suffered in large, impersonal schools. Vivienne's elementary-school experience was a destructive one. Bookish, plump and sarcastic, sensitive and stubborn, she learned as a small child what it was like to be different and lonely. The transition from family to school can be a traumatic one. For the child between five and twelve years the new community has the character of another home where self-esteem is at stake and the rules are strange. It is during these years that the news from the outside world comes in. You're too fat, too thin, too short, too tall. Your clothes are stupid. You smell. You aren't going to be invited to the birthday party. No one will play with you at recess. Even for those who escape such harsh judgments, the world of elementary school can be an uneasy one.

Large schools can dehumanize their teachers. Even the most well-intentioned have little time to pause and consider any single child's struggle with self-acceptance. Vivienne's school was, I assume, much like other big elementary schools of its time. I remember my own five children and how carefully each chose and laid out the night before, the clothes for the first day of school. I delivered each one of them to rules against talking, to the institutional halls and the cutouts that passed for art. And I remember how each one returned in the afternoons more humorless and tired. I remember, too, the "party" in first grade a parent had furnished for the birthday of one of the children. Each desk had been supplied with one cupcake and two candies. Not allowed to chat, the thirty children sat somberly in their places, each one eating the party food obediently and joylessly. The teacher sat sorting through papers at her desk.

In creative writing classes, my students often remember their early school experiences. Jackie described an impressive lesson in mistrust:

It was during one of those spelling lessons that acci- dently an incoming note to me . . . was caught by Miss Oliver. . . . I knew I was doomed. She kept staring at me and then she slowly walked up to my desk and motioned for me to give the note to her. . . . Her face was shaped like something between an olive and a chipmunk. One side of her face drooped with an excessive amount of skin, making her look like she had a pouch. Her slightly yellow stained teeth protruded. . . .

I even remember that she was wearing a black and white tweed skirt that just covered her fleshy, lumpy knees. She had on a white, woolen, stretchy turtle neck: the kind you always wish elderly ladies wouldn't wear because . . . their bosoms are much too saggy and rolls of fat bulge out at their waistlines. . . .

What the note actually said was, "Jackie, I'm bored silly. Goddamit. I wish spelling would go to hell." . . .

She was getting angrier and angrier . . . with a half-con- trolled yell she screamed, "Whoever wrote this note, I wish you would be honest enough to tell me this instant!"

Peter shyly raised his hand. A sort of put-on toughness crept over his face.

I knew what was to happen. I felt terribly sick. . . .

"Peter, open your mouth."

Peter, the small, freckle-faced Texan boy, opened his mouth, revealing even white teeth.

"You can take a bigger bite than that," she angrily re- marked as she shoved the new white cake of Ivory soap back into his mouth.

A few tiny flakes of soap fell onto his red plaid shirt.

Tears had started streaming down my face. I saw a blurred figure rush out the door, little Ivory soap flakes falling behind him. Our spelling lesson resumed but now I could concentrate even less...had Peter cried yet?... had Peter cried yet?

Such events, of course, should never happen. But they do. Sometimes English classes provide a healing forum where young people can compare experiences and become more self-accepting. They can leave, for a moment, the emphasis on achievement and test scores and share what's really crucial to them: their inner development.

A great deal of important learning goes on in these early grades that is not a part of any written curriculum. What does the teacher think of them? What are the unspoken rules? Kate, with an irony reminiscent of Vivienne, remembers a second-grade history lesson:

AMERICAN HISTORY LESSON — BENEDICT ARNOLD
What difference does it make he died ashamed,
Old and banished with his uniform on?
No one will forgive you now, old man,
Not my whole second grade class.
Miss Getty with the sweat stains on her dress,
Insists we know, white fat legs crossed and veined,
That you were sorry and you died ashamed.

No-one is allowed to love a traitor —
Not in my class nor any other after it.
All the wondering children will be shown:
We find it fitting that you died alone.

No one is allowed to love a traitor. In second grade, children believe what they are told and apply it to themselves. There can be no forgiveness for those who break rules. The lesson sinks deep. The more compliant children take no risks; they often perform well, as Vivienne did. By all the standards of testing and lesson goals, Vivienne scored high. But her critical inner despair went unnoticed. While impersonal schools harm all of their students with this crucial lack of communication, the Viviennes are lost and their injuries compounded. "If anything," writes Arnold Madison in *Suicide and Young People,* "we *all* must share in the blame for poor communication and understanding . . . for in truth, they are the immediate causes of suicide." [3] Large institutions continue to run the risk of ignoring depressed young people at precisely the moment when an aware adult might help.

There were aware adults in the Cambridge Friends community when Vivienne went there in sixth grade. As her mother said, "Vivienne blossomed." It's not hard to see why. John May was the first teacher to look upon Vivienne with warmth and compassion. Cambridge Friends offered Vivienne her first sympathetic school environment. She, at last, made friendships in her age group. Her intellectual and creative powers were recognized and valued. Her self-esteem rose. She had someone to turn to.

John was a young teacher. An idealist, fulfilling his alternate service as a draft objector, newly come to the East, he found himself uneasy in the Harvard-oriented atmosphere of Cambridge. One can imagine that he took special comfort in his warm student relationships — a legitimate reward of teaching. While John gave Vivienne a new view of herself, it was a tragedy for both of them that she had encountered no other adults who could respond vividly to her. In a productive school, many teachers should offer the adolescent support and respect in varied and individual ways.

John May represented to Vivienne one important aspect of that "second chance" Freud describes that all adolescents have to reintegrate old experiences and initiate new ones. In this way teachers are, perhaps, even more important to adolescents than they are to any other age group. They have the power to inspire or render cynical. Teachers can encourage and enable, wither and humiliate. They can recognize and value. They can simply listen. Their daily relationships with students include more time and varieties of experience than any other professional can command. An effective teacher, as Martin Buber remarks, is "a really existing man ... present to his pupils: he educates through contact." When teaching goes well, the teacher is able, as Norman Kiell observes, "through some special, indefinable gift ... not only to bring life to the high drama of ideas but also to bring out within the individual his best efforts." What is this "special, indefinable gift"? Carl Rogers describes it: " ... Significant learning rests upon certain attitudinal qualities which exist in the personal *relationship* between the facilitator and the learner.... Perhaps the most basic of these essential attitudes is realness or genuineness." [4] Did John May have it?

Here was a young man who not only valued Vivienne's talent but was interested in her well-being. He noticed her shyness. She felt his sympathy and personal warmth. From what we know of John through Vivienne, he was both "present" and "genuine." He "brought life" to the ideals of kindness between people and openness in their exchanges. He certainly allowed Vivienne "to make her best efforts" and contributed, however briefly, to her self-acceptance. Adolescents, with their contradictory vigilance for hypocrisy, are always ready to idealize. Vivienne idealized John May.

No one is immune to such flattery. We can imagine that John enjoyed his success with the children of the sixth grade. Sincere and inventive in his teaching, he seemed, too, to have a special instinct for their needs. But the occupational hazard of teaching is vanity, sometimes truly unconscious, and a growing taste for the power of ruling the universe of a class. Teachers, always in a position of authority, are often the objects of uncritical affection. They tend, like their charges, to idealism and are more than usually interested in questions of personal growth. Perhaps teachers have a special identification with young people as a result of their own striking experiences in adolescence. There are said to be selective factors in our choice of vocation. Lawyers may be middle children with a permanent concern for balance and justice. Ministers can be those who have difficulty making close personal relationships. We teachers seem to be attracted to the turmoil of the maturing process. John May was certainly sensitive to Vivienne's need for self-regard.

But relationships are never simple and John May was to face a situation Peter Blos describes in *The Adolescent Personality:* "Adolescent behaviour is unstable, inconsistent and unpredictable. Teachers are confronted with a shifting situation that is often difficult to handle." [5] In handling this kind of pressure, the most effective teachers become more flexible, the least successful more rigid. Some simply flounder. When teachers are uncomfortable, some may turn against the students and start putting excessive emphasis on "respect" and "discipline." Others may drop the boundaries between adult and child and become the slightly more educated teenager in the group. It is a difficult task, even for the most seasoned.

It takes a tough and realistic self-regard with a special sympathy for the age group to spend all day with adolescents. They are seductive and challenging. They are watchful, adoring, critical and scornful. They can be dramatic, selfish, apathetic and passively resistant. It is not always easy to establish the line between child and adult, between sympathy and responsibility, between fantasy and reality.

In the arena of the classroom, all teachers demonstrate their own past experiences. They are, like the young people they teach, the result of these experiences, no less influenced than their students by their own unconscious aims. Therefore we have the scholar who pleased his teacher in classical studies; the disciplinarian who was himself subject to goading and scorn; the aesthete who won special notice for his cleverness with symbolism; the philosopher who was praised for his discernment of universal themes; the outcast who woos friendships denied him in his own school days; the inhibited loner, compelled to make provocative allusions in class. While these are pardonable quirks and present in every profession, they have a special impact on adolescent development. Young people can be more affected by adult models than by academic content. They seek the maturity and enthusiasm of adults with strong ideas and visions worth sharing. They look for integrity and the creative energy that comes with experience and competence. For a while John May served in this role for Vivienne and she "blossomed."

Vivienne encountered John May; what's equally interesting to teachers, John May encountered Vivienne.

A westerner in the East, chilled by New England winter and sensitive to his own notion of educational status — San Francisco State as compared to Harvard, for example — John must have welcomed the uncritical affection offered him. But he was young and naive. Somewhere along the line, he failed to grasp the "shifting situation." The boundaries of relationships with young people must always be drawn by adults. The responsibility of every mature friend is to reflect reality as kindly as possible. But John May was inexperienced and he did not recognize his own limitations. He was largely unaware of the profundity of his importance to Vivienne. Although he consciously sought to raise her self-esteem, he did not guess that her dependence upon him for equilibrium was becoming crucial.

In fact, Vivienne's "blossoming" was not firmly rooted. Although in sixth grade she treasured his comment that she was beautiful, she chronically doubted his regard, and her friendships at school were eroded by jealousy and feelings of worthlessness. Much of this John May knew.

Vivienne denied her love for John. Her poem, for example, written the summer after sixth grade, "Take My Hand," reveals the depth of her attachment to John, but Vivienne insisted that it had a more universal meaning. This was true, too, of the letter she and another girl wrote in the winter of their seventh-grade year. They wanted to tell John May that they loved him. "Not 'love' love, but admiration and consideration and friendship love." In a postscript Vivienne added, "It seems as though you may like me, but you probably don't *love* me. And *I* do love you." She quickly switched it to mean love in general: "But I hope that someday I'm loved as much as you are." The disguise, however, didn't work. The letter ends, "P.S. When I finished talking to you tonight, I walked into the dining room and cried. Why??" John replied that the compliment made him feel "super good. So often people don't tell each other of the good things. . . . I admire you both very much also."

Life as we live it is unaccompanied by signposts. The script in the writing is far more tenuous than the script completed. How was John to respond to Vivienne's obvious crush on him? Could he know how seriously her self-esteem depended on his responses to her? Was the answer that her compliment made him feel "super good" overly (though unwittingly) seductive? Did his turning of the word "love" into an avowal of admiration respond appropriately to her message? In the light of what happened next, we can look back upon this communication as a milestone worth noting, but only retrospect provides us with the insight. At the time, we can imagine, it seemed simply an excessive declaration of a devoted student. Perhaps it even seemed an extension of John's own allegiance to warm and open exchanges. In April of 1972, Vivienne's emotions were more in conflict. John May was, as Peter Blos put it, "confronted with a shifting situation."

The news that John would be leaving the following year led Vivienne to critical thoughts about his "shell." High-school teachers often experience hostility from students who sense a forthcoming loss. In fact, the cycle is not new. Children reject their parents for teachers and other adults outside the family, high-school seniors feel newly critical of faculty in favor of the next step into college. "Senioritis" is traditionally a response to the approaching graduation and separation from school. Thoughtful teachers try to support the transition. While "senioritis" may include genuine restlessness and a wish to move on, when school has been an enabling experience, we intuitively feel the rejection as part of the introductory inner work necessary for leaving. So Vivienne seems to have, at first, prepared herself for John May's dreaded absence from Cambridge Friends.

Depression was soon to follow, and although John continued to try to boost Vivienne's self-esteem in the same ways that were once successful, she thought she was "developing a strong inferiority complex." Was this "An old forgotten sword... / Suddenly glistening and sharp!" in her poem of that time, "Patterns of My Lifetime"? Again we pause and wonder if John should have regarded these expressions as warning signals.

Self-hatred and aloneness are not remarkable among sensitive teenagers, but they are always clues that an adolescent can benefit from understanding teachers. Parents, who represent too much of the early world of dependency, are often helpless. Teachers can bring a sense of perspective and patience to the embattled young person. They can, in effect, acknowledge and moderate the cruel self-criticism. This is especially important at a time when adolescents are too proud and perhaps too ashamed to confide in their peers. Before friends, they have an urgent need to appear "normal." I am always impressed in writing classes that students sitting side by side, isolated and fearful of scorn, express identical anguish and self-doubt, each imagining the other immune to misery. It seems to be a part of the developmental struggle.

Had Vivienne never known John May, she probably would have suffered depression for other causes. One can imagine her idealizing a disappointing friend of Rob's, for example, or transferring her needs to still another teacher. Given the universality of Vivienne's painful search, a question does arise about school environments and whether they afford genuine opportunities for young people to build self-belief and independence. In a symposium on schools and suicide, held some seventy years ago and presided over by Sigmund Freud, Dr. Edward Stekel observed:

> The school should help its pupils in that period when their sandcastles collapse and life brutally shows them the impossibility of reaching their fantasies. The child and the neurotic perish from the irreality of their fantasies.... Teachers have failed to guide their pupils from the world of fantasy into that of life ... the schools should seek to lead the child gently, so to speak, playfully, from the realm of fantasy into real life — not with empty formulas, accusatives and infinitives, algebraic lumber and confusing masses of dates, not with harsh examinations and tortuous grammar. It should know how to awaken the child's senses to the riches of life and nature, the imperishable masterpieces of ancient and modern art, and indeed all the achievements of human civilization.[6]

Could Vivienne's needs for self-esteem have been met in other ways, broadened so that they didn't focus so dangerously on one teacher? Could school have awakened her "senses to the riches of life and nature"? Could all young people benefit from a different view of their education? Freud himself, in that same seminar on schools and suicide, had his own vision of an appropriate atmosphere:

> ... A secondary school should achieve more than not driving its pupils to suicide. It should give them a desire

to live and should offer them support and backing at a time of life at which the conditions of their development compel them to relax ties with their parental home and their family. It seems to be indisputable that schools fail in this, and in many respects fall short of their duty of providing a substitute for the family and of arousing interest in the life of the world outside. . . . The school must never forget that it has to deal with immature individuals who cannot be denied a right to linger at certain stages of development and even at certain disagreeable ones. The school must not take on itself the inexorable quality of life: it must not seek to be more than a *game* of life.[7]

Even in the most well-intentioned schools there is still a debate about the "game of life." Cambridge is a private and therefore privileged school. We have a gifted faculty dedicated to the welfare of students. Nevertheless, we sometimes sit in faculty meetings, balancing our Styrofoam cups of coffee, and argue about "rigor," "academic standards," "discipline," "requirements," "penalties," "the grading system." There are those who assert that classes ought to be "demanding" and should seek to discipline students for their inevitable entrance into a competitive and heartless society. They generally take pride in the marking system, exams and exacting homework. They are vigilant lest their students "waste time." They view more "progressive" teachers as anarchistic. They often admire subjects taught "in order." At the other extreme are the "permissive" teachers whose courses tend to be hazily designed and who prize excitement and action in their classrooms. They pose provocative questions and sometimes ignore historical background in favor of a contemporary view. They sometimes depend too heavily on "student motivation." They are advocates of "theme" and "insight." Their students sometimes find them confusingly abstract. Such teachers view their debaters as "traditional" and "rigid."

Each extreme eliminates an important adolescent need. The first, "traditional" view ignores a pressing issue for young people: independence. The system tends to keep them subservient to authority. It punishes error and leaves no room for exploration and personal risk-taking. It never honors the right "to linger at certain stages." The second, "progressive" attitude errs in another way. It too neglects a pressing adolescent requirement: leadership. Young people need, indeed hunger for, compelling models. The "progressive" method doesn't seem to offer enough "support and backing at a time of life at which the conditions ... compel them [adolescents] to relax ties with their parental home." We have not yet established the setting for young people that would truly foster growth.

The latest government report on youth (ordered by President Nixon) calls schools "an inappropriate setting for nearly all objectives involving responsibility that affect others ... as these are important to the transition to adulthood ... schools act to retard youth." The report goes on to propose a change in the notion of schools, suggesting more experimental education, more flexibility in curriculum, more mixtures of actual work and study, better arrangements for young people to assume responsibility for others — such as day-care centers in schools. The report would like to see schools include "responsibilities for his [the student's] own welfare and others ... orientation to productive and responsible tasks, learning through action and experience ... not by being taught.... To reduce the isolation of youth from adults and from productive tasks in society ... to bring about a greater degree of responsibility of adults for the development of youth." [8]

Certainly we get a sense that Vivienne was too isolated and that her resources for self-esteem were too limited. Could she have gained her balance in that mythical school the Nixon report describes? Is there something wrong in even our most adventurous school settings?

But schools themselves are not entirely to blame. Societies

generally design the educational systems they need and want.
Our society seems to impose a business model on our schools.
Students are placed in competitive situations with one another
as though each individual were a profit-making organization.
At a time when young people seek their own self-acceptance
through friendships, we pit them against each other. In the
stage when adolescents need to identify with adults, we subject
most of them to large schools and impersonal and authoritative
teachers. We take the unready and forming personality, full of
its own uncertainties and doubts, and require proof of its "earn-
ing power." Our courses seem aimed at a "final product."
Vivienne's first six school years were spent in such institutions.

By the time Vivienne went to Cambridge Friends School,
she had been injured and there were more injuries to come.
The years of her short adolescence seemed particularly painful
ones in our history. She responded with personal anguish to
Watergate, American Indian problems, hijacking.

Like Vivienne's, my own adolescence was a privileged one,
but we were born into different generations. When I was an
adolescent the community was more stable and the news more
muted. The radio was full of the adventures of Jack Armstrong
and, although people were certainly killed, death was not served
up as entertainment. Mr. Greeninger's drugstore always smelled
of vanilla and he could be counted on to open the pharmacy at
midnight if my mother had an emergency. I went to school
with his son Ned. My grandparents lived with us. My aunts
and uncles were only a brisk walk away. My father's siblings
called him "Brother" and I grew up with cousins who always
addressed him as "Uncle Brother." Strangers were noted in our
neighborhood and only my old aunt May, who had never gotten
over the death of Baby Rose, took drugs.

Aunt Claire, my mother's sister, knew everything: how to get
grass stains out of a white shirt; what subway to take for obscure
points in town; which shoes were practical and worth the

money. It was always Aunt Claire who came when you were sick or sad.

My parents' friends had all attended school and college together and we called them Aunt and Uncle, though they were no blood relation. They came on our vacation sometimes where the oceans were always fresh and the air seemed pure and limitless. No one spoke of nitrites in the morning bacon or hormones in the Sunday roast. In our adolescent eyes, the world seemed safe and dependable. Couples celebrated golden wedding anniversaries and rarely moved from their houses.

Personal experiences have changed for adolescents. Divorce rates have soared. A family can move halfway across the country at a moment's notice and those that stay together are unusual. I notice this especially since I teach in a boarding school. More than half our students need two sets of grades and comments. I Xerox the required copies and send them to fathers in distant cities and mothers with new names. Sometimes, for our students, there is no one to turn to and so they often turn to each other to trade whatever physical closeness or substance they can. While adolescence has always been a time of change and anxiety, the outside world offers them little comfort. Young people seem more drastically unhappy, cynical and hopeless than they did even twenty years ago. The shrinking universe, the unthinkable possibility of nuclear war and the failing economy have all poisoned their future. The inner world of adolescence is difficult enough. When the impact of changing societies is added to it, young people sometimes flounder.

Even family deaths were once shared in ways that made the loss seem less personal and poignant. Ralphie was our family doctor. He had gone to school with my father. He was there the night my cousin Donald died from what we thought was a cold. We arrived in that chilled and fractured dawn to find Ralphie in the living room, weeping with Aunt Prue. My old aunt May could not be told at once. She was considered too fragile for the news. And so all that morning I heard my mother telephone at fifteen-minute intervals to say, "Donald is very sick," "Donald is worse," "Donald is failing," until at one terrible moment she was able to say, "Donald died." And in my eyes, my cousin Donald, leaning his bike against a tree in my front yard the week before, crumpled and fell.

But it was different for my own children and for Vivienne. I remember, for example, when they were small, how President Kennedy died again and again on the evening news, how he clutched his throat and slumped in the limousine. Nightly newscasts showed our own uniformed young men burning villages, the hosing of black civil-rights workers, police attacking students, and reports on the shooting of Allison Krause at Kent State University after she had placed a flower in the barrel of a National Guardsman's gun. Television brought brutality into our living room. Adolescents are particularly vulnerable to the hurts of others, although they sometimes seem impervious. They lack the hardening and the protection more typical of adults. Tyche, for example, wrote in a ninth-grade journal:

> ... I just looked up to see Louisa's bloody finger. . . . It started me thinking about being at someone's house on Friday and he pulled out this old Civil War sword. Everyone thought it was really neat ... but it made me feel sick and horrible — my stomach got all funny — when I thought of him so easily taking that sword and thrusting it through one of their stomachs ... God! That's what scares me so much ... all the violence in the world. Everywhere!
>
> I used to think, and still try to think, that the world is based around love, unity and harmony ... but then I think that in everyone there always is and always has been, greed ...

While it would be fruitless to argue against the instant communication television offers, it is tempting to remember the days when we awoke more gradually to the battles of the world. In those days we seemed to have more time to strengthen. We were temporarily buffered. But Vivienne had little protection from the world's violence. And there was no real community to comfort her.

Vivienne's most important resource, John May, seemed to sustain her. But by the fall of her eighth-grade year, as John's departure neared, school seemed like "a drag" and she was deeply lonely.

After John left, Vivienne mentioned suicide more seriously, but felt so worthless she wondered, "How can you kill nothing?" In June she wrote to John and asked him to "send me something encouraging... for me to live on for a while." A month later she wrote him about her attempt to strangle herself.

Here we pause in alarm. John didn't reply immediately. When he did write, he commented on her "tough" time and advised her to find someone to cry with. While this might be useful advice for ordinary depression, it doesn't respond directly to Vivienne's suicide attempt, or to the gravity of her entire situation. John May was the only adult who knew of Vivienne's critical despair. Retrospect tempts us to rewrite history.

What if John had called Vivienne from California and told her that he could not keep her dangerous secret? What if he had phoned Paulette and warned her to ignore Vivienne's injunction against reading her journal? Could we revise the awful outcome?

But life is not like the movies. The reel can't be run again. What was it actually like for John? Did he feel, as Laurel did, bound by Vivienne's confidence? Did he hope her strangulation attempt was merely a dramatic gesture, meant to demonstrate her sadness? Did he feel her confession would serve as a relief and prevent her further acting out?

All of this certainly crosses a teacher's mind when a student shares tragic thoughts. Empathetic teachers are aware of the pride and dignity, the sense of privacy young people feel so keenly. Here, indeed, is that puzzling line that teachers sometimes face between themselves and other professionals. When should a teacher report troubling news? When would it drive a wedge between him and the adolescent who trusts no one else? Can any sympathetic adult handle the situation?

Knowing what we know now, the answer seems simple. Vivienne tried to strangle herself. John May was in over his head. The family should have been alerted. A therapist should have been called in.

But, in my experience, these are not easy decisions. We hesitate to cut lines of communication that may, in the end, help to heal. The strangulation description in Vivienne's letter is followed by "I have decided to stick this life of mine out," and she went on to report that she was writing poetry again.

These are reassuring communications and seem to put the suicidal impulse in the past. One can imagine that John May's vote of confidence and his advice about handling further "tough" times were addressed to the healthy part of Vivienne, which he hoped to support. Can you force a teenager to seek counseling? Should John have called the family and suggested hospitalization? Perhaps he felt that this might dangerously alarm her and precipitate another suicidal gesture. He might have hesitated to treat her as "sick."

The issues are difficult ones. Adolescents don't seem to be the best candidates for therapy. They tend to see adult counselors as official parental representatives and consequently as a threat to their unsteady independence. They often lack, too, the deep and continuing discontent that informs the motivation of older people. It is hard for them to commit themselves seriously to regular appointments. They are inclined to flee when sessions come closest to the heart of their suffering. They would rather turn to trusted teachers or other adults when they need a listener. They prefer to remain in control of the time and the extent of their own confidences.

But this poses another problem. Teachers have their limitations. They may be frightened of emotional crises. They may mistake what they are hearing. They may lack the personal insight and training that illuminate for psychologists, not only the meaning of confidences young people offer, but, perhaps even more important, their own blind spots and denials. Teachers are not professional psychologists. They need to know when to turn to the experts. There is a distinct line between what the counseling profession offers and what educators can do to prevent suicide.

The distinction between the two is entirely proper. In some ways, teachers represent reality and daily partnership. A teacher may see as "lazy" what a psychiatrist would label "paralyzed." A teacher could respond to "hostility" where a psychologist would see "depression." Young people need to know both aspects of themselves: the effect of their behavior and, when it is troubling, the emotional logic that causes it. Perhaps these two functions cannot be blended in one person, but it is safe to say that the two viewpoints ought to come closer together and that teachers should make new relationships with counselors.

In our school we have a training group for teachers, now in its fourth year. We meet once a week for two hours under the supervision of an experienced psychologist. There we talk about ourselves, our students, relationships and events that puzzle us. The group serves to enlighten and inform us, deepen our personal insight and enrich our understanding of young people. We can better recognize and handle normal adolescent turmoil. It does not, however, make us psychologists, and we learn to be very respectful of that line between us.

The training group has had some effect on our courses. We feel a new responsibility to expose young people to experiences in the real world while we can still provide a forum for discussion and evaluation. In a ninth-grade class this year, we attended court sessions and could see at first hand that the structure for balance and order still existed. Older students spend a month off campus in jobs and apprenticeships and then come back to us to share their discoveries. Our program includes an oral-history experiment, and a study of the Holocaust from original documents. We try to provide perspective on the violence our students observe. I have been especially aware of this since Vivienne's death.

In that last summer John May had some reason to feel that Vivienne was on safe ground again. Although she shared many of her worries, they were the normal concerns of growing up and there were, too, spirited accounts of square dances and plays. It wasn't until August 22 that the next alarming event took place.

Vivienne wrote to John that she had taken pills during "a really selfish streak" and that she had done this on impulse during a fight with Laurel.

Vivienne never got a reply to this letter and perhaps it was because she wrote the very next day a chatty and reasonably cheerful account of her experience with sex and marijuana and of renovation plans for the house in Gloucester. He must have been comforted, too, to realize that this time the entire family knew of Vivienne's pill incident and that the responsibility was not only his. He did not guess that they dismissed it as a childish exercise in anger. The trouble was that the Loomises lacked John's background about Vivienne's suicidal impulses and he didn't share it with them.

The Cambridge School started. Vivienne found the teachers less personal in her new school. Beginning students sometimes wish for immediate relationships to take the place of old ones. Vivienne had a particularly urgent need to substitute for John May. That year the faculty at Cambridge School was preoccupied with its new module system. Every course had been newly designed. Although, had she stayed longer, Vivienne might have found someone to turn to, the beginning months of the school year had an air of crisis and excitement for the teachers, and they were more than usually involved in planning. My own brief encounter with her was a good example. I would ordinarily have sought Vivienne out, in spite of her reticence with me, but I remember being on my way to a lunch-hour curriculum committee that day on the path. And in the days that followed, my schedule was filled with the demands of the new module system. In the first nine weeks at our school, Vivienne found no adult she could feel close to. Once again she turned to John May in early December. The letter she wrote him on December 2 had a new tone. It was not only deeply depressed, alarmingly suicidal, but it had a frightening resignation. She had nowhere to go and crying offered her no relief. Family counseling left her feeling like "the most destructive factor." As it turned out, John received this communication after her death.

Vivienne died at fourteen. No one close to her was able to keep her from suicide. As Marianne Moore wrote, "What is our innocence, / what is our guilt? All are / naked, none is safe." Shaken and changed, we review Vivienne's suffering and reconsider the plight of adolescents everywhere. Her death reminds us again: all children are under our care.

Notes

INTRODUCTION

1. A. Alvarez, *The Savage God* (London: Weidenfeld and Nicolson, 1971), p. 90.
2. Jerry Jacobs, *Adolescent Suicide* (New York: John Wiley and Sons, 1971), p. 107.
3. Albert Camus, *The Myth of Sisyphus and Other Essays* (New York: Alfred A. Knopf, 1955), p. 4.
4. Sigmund Freud, "Mourning and Melancholia," in *The Standard Edition of Complete Psychological Works*, vol. 14 (London: Hogarth Press, 1957), p. 252.

A CLINICIAN'S ANALYSIS

1. Walker Percy, *The Last Gentleman* (New York: Avon, 1978), p. 291.
2. James Carroll, *The Winter Name of God* (Kansas City: Sheed and Ward, 1975), p. 87; Albert Camus, *The Myth of Sisyphus and Other Essays* (New York: Alfred A. Knopf, 1955), p. 3.
3. Jean Baechler, *Suicides*, translated by Barry Cooper (New York: Basic Books, 1979), p. xx.
4. Peter Blos, *On Adolescence: A Psychoanalytic Interpretation* (New York: Free Press of Glencoe, 1962), pp. 94, 96.
5. Quotations from family members and Anne Tucker are taken from tape-recorded interviews conducted by the authors in 1977 and 1978.
6. A. Alvarez, *The Savage God* (London: Weidenfeld and Nicolson, 1971), p. 89.
7. Carl Malmquist, "Depressions in Childhood and Adolescence," *New England Journal of Medicine* 284(16):887–893, 284(17):955–691.

8. Van Spruiell, "Narcissistic Transformations in Adolescence," *International Journal of Psychoanalytic Psychotherapy* 4:528 (1975).
9. Edward Bibring, "The Mechanism of Depression," in P. Greenacre, ed., *Affective Disorders* (New York: International Universities Press, 1953), p. 26.
10. Malmquist, p. 891.
11. Ibid.
12. Anaïs Nin, *The Diary of Anaïs Nin,* vol. 1 (New York: Harcourt, Brace and World, 1966), p. 115.
13. Ibid., p. 299.
14. Nancy Cotten, "The Development of Self-Esteem and Self-Esteem Regulation," to be published by International Universities Press.
15. Malmquist, p. 891.
16. H. Kohut, *The Analysis of the Self* (New York: International Universities Press, 1971), p. 25.
17. Samuel Ritvo, "Late Adolescence: Developmental and Clinical Considerations," *Psychoanalytic Study of the Child* 26:241–263 (1971).
18. Peter Barglow and Margaret Schaeffer, "The Fate of the Feminine Self in Normative Adolescent Regression," in Max Sugar, ed., *Female Adolescent Development* (New York: Brunner/Mazel, 1979), p. 206.
19. Blos, *On Adolescence,* p. 95.
20. Henry A. Murray, "Dead to the World: The Passions of Herman Melville," in E. S. Shneidman, ed., *Essays in Self-Destruction* (New York: Science House, 1967), p. 11.
21. Sigmund Freud, "Mourning and Melancholia," in *The Standard Edition of Complete Psychological Works,* vol. 14 (London: Hogarth Press, 1957), p. 306.
22. Otto Fenichel, *Psychoanalytic Theory of Neurosis* (New York: Norton, 1945), p. 400.
23. Bibring, "The Mechanism of Depression," pp. 13–48.
24. George Bernanos, *Mouchette,* translated by J. C. Whitehouse (New York: Holt, Rinehart and Winston, 1966).
25. Nin, pp. 243, 223, 224.
26. Deaths and Death Rates for Suicide, Mortality Statistics Branch, Division of Vital Statistics, National Center for Health Statistics, *Vital Statistics of the United States,* vol. 2: *Mortality* (published and unpublished data); "Teen-age Suicide," *Newsweek,* August 28, 1978.
27. Emile Durkheim, *Suicide* (reprinted, New York: Free Press, 1951), p. 26.
28. Gregory Zilboorg, "Considerations on Suicide with Particular Reference to That of the Young," *American Journal of Orthopsychiatry* 7:18 (1937).
29. Paul Friedman, "An Individual Act," in E. S. Shneidman, ed., *On the Nature of Suicide* (San Francisco: Jossey-Bass, 1969), pp. 51–52.
30. Max Warren, "On Suicide," *Journal of the American Psychoanalytic Association* 24(1):228 (1976).
31. Francine Klagsbrun, *Youth and Suicide: Too Young to Die* (New York: Pocket Books, 1977), p. 37.
32. Frank Schulsinger et al., "A Family Study of Suicide," in M. Schou

and E. Strömgren, eds., *Origin, Prevention and Treatment of Affective Disorders* (London and New York: Academic Press, 1979), pp. 277–287.

33. Personal communication from S. S. Kety, April 6, 1981.
34. Charles R. Shaw and Ruth F. Schelkun, "Suicidal Behavior in Children," *Psychiatry* 28:159 (1965).
35. James M. Toolan, "Suicide in Children and Adolescents," *American Journal of Psychotherapy* 29(3):341 (1975).
36. George Engel, "Anxiety and Depression-Withdrawal: The Primary Affects of Unpleasure," *International Journal of Psychoanalysis* 43:89–98 (1962); James E. Anthony, "Childhood Depression," in James E. Anthony and Therese Benedek, eds., *Depression and Human Existence* (Boston: Little, Brown, 1975), p. 245.
37. Stephen A. Applebaum and Philip S. Holzman, "The Color-Shading Response and Suicide," *Journal of Projective Techniques* 26:160 (1962).
38. Herbert Hendin, "Student Suicide: Death as a Life Cycle," *Journal of Nervous and Mental Diseases* 160:204–219 (1975).
39. Zilboorg, "Considerations on Suicide with Particular Reference to That of the Young," p. 22.
40. See John P. Miller, "Suicide and Adolescence," *Adolescence* 10:15 (1975).
41. James M. Toolan, "Suicide and Suicidal Attempts in Children and Adolescents," *American Journal of Psychiatry* 118:723 (1962); Joseph D. Teicher and Jerry Jacobs, "Adolescents Who Attempt Suicide: Preliminary Findings," *American Journal of Psychiatry* 122:1252 (1966).
42. Nin, p. 128.
43. A. Haim, *Adolescent Suicide* (New York: International Universities Press, 1974), p. 257; Robert Litman, "Sigmund Freud and Suicide," in E. S. Shneidman, ed., *Essays in Self-Destruction* (New York: Science House, 1967), p. 340.
44. Friedman, "An Individual Act," pp. 49–50.
45. Klagsbrun, *Youth and Suicide*, p. 134.
46. Baechler, *Suicides*, p. 53.
47. Antonin Artaud, *Antonin Artaud Anthology*, edited by Jack Hirschman (San Francisco: City Lights Books, 1965), p. 56.
48. Maurice Friedman et al., "Attempted Suicide and Self-Mutilation in Adolescence: Some Direct Observations from a Psychoanalytic Research Project," *International Journal of Psychoanalysis* 53:179–184 (1972).
49. Ake Mattsson, Lynne R. Seese, and James W. Hawkins, "Suicidal Behavior as a Child Psychiatric Emergency," *Archives of General Psychiatry* 20:100–109 (1969).
50. Toolan, "Suicide and Suicidal Attempts in Children and Adolescents."
51. Baechler, *Suicides*, p. 63.
52. Jerry Jacobs, *Adolescent Suicide* (New York: John Wiley and Sons, 1971), p. 21.
53. Heiman Van Damm, remarks at interdisciplinary colloquium on teenage suicide, American Psychoanalytic Association, New York City, December 17, 1978.

Bibliography

Alvarez, A. *The Savage God*. London: Weidenfeld and Nicolson, 1971.

Anthony, James E. "Childhood Depression." In *Depression and Human Existence*, edited by James E. Anthony and Therese Benedek. Boston: Little, Brown, 1975.

Applebaum, Stephen A., and Holzman, Philip S. "The Color-Shading Response and Suicide." *Journal of Projective Techniques* 26:155–161 (1962).

Artaud, Antonin. *Antonin Artaud Anthology*. Edited by Jack Hirschman. San Francisco: City Lights Books, 1965.

Baechler, Jean. *Suicides*. Translated from the French by Barry Cooper. New York: Basic Books, 1979.

Barglow, Peter, and Schaeffer, Margaret. "The Fate of the Feminine Self in Normative Adolescent Regression." In *Female Adolescent Development*, edited by Max Sugar. New York: Brunner/Mazel, 1979.

Bernanos, Georges. *Mouchette*. Translated from the French by J. C. Whitehouse. New York: Holt, Rinehart and Winston, 1966. (Published in 1937 with French title *Nouvelle Histoire de Mouchette*.)

Bibring, Edward. "The Mechanism of Depression." In *Affective Disorders*, edited by P. Greenacre. New York: International Universities Press, 1953.

Blos, Peter. *The Adolescent Personality*. New York: Appleton-Century, 1941.

———. *On Adolescence: A Psychoanalytic Interpretation*. New York: Free Press of Glencoe, 1962.

———. *The Adolescent Passage: Developmental Issues*. New York: International Universities Press, 1979.

Boor, Myron. "Anomie and U.S. Suicide Rates, 1973–1976." *Journal of Clinical Psychology* 35(4):703–706 (1979).

Cain, Albert C., ed. *Survivors of Suicide*. Springfield: Charles C. Thomas, 1972.

Camus, Albert. *The Myth of Sisyphus and Other Essays.* New York: Alfred A. Knopf, 1955.

Carlson, Gabrielle A., and Cantwell, Dennia P. "Unmasking Masked Depression in Children and Adolescents." *American Journal of Psychiatry* 137:445–449 (1980).

Carroll, James. *The Winter Name of God.* Kansas City: Sheed and Ward, 1975.

Cavan, Ruth Shonle. *Suicide.* New York: Russell and Russell, 1928.

Daston, Paul G., and Sakheim, George A. "Prediction of Successful Suicide from the Rorschach Test, Using a Sign Approach." *Journal of Projective Techniques* 24:355–361 (1960).

Durkheim, Emile. *Suicide.* Reprint. New York: Free Press, 1951.

Engel, George. "Anxiety and Depression-Withdrawal: The Primary Affects of Unpleasure." *International Journal of Psycho-Analysis* 43:89–98 (1962).

Farberow, Norman L. "Bibliography on Suicide and Suicide Prevention: 1897–1967." Washington, D.C.: U.S. Government Printing Office, 1969.

Farberow, Norman L., and Shneidman, Edwin S. *The Cry for Help.* New York: McGraw-Hill, 1961.

Feinstein, Sherman C. "Adolescent Depression." *Depression and Human Existence,* edited by James E. Anthony and Therese Benedek. Boston: Little, Brown, 1975.

Fenichel, Otto. *Psychoanalytic Theory of Neurosis.* New York: Norton, 1945.

Finch, Stuart M., and Poznanski, Elva O. *Adolescent Suicide.* Springfield: Charles C. Thomas, 1971.

Freud, Sigmund. "Some Reflections on Schoolboy Psychology" (1914). In *The Standard Edition of Complete Psychological Works,* vol. 13. Edited by James Strachey et al. London: Hogarth Press, 1957.

———. "On Narcissism: An Introduction" (1914). In *The Standard Edition of Complete Psychological Works,* vol. 14. Edited by James Strachey et al. London: Hogarth Press, 1957.

———. "Mourning and Melancholia" (1917[1915]). In *The Standard Edition of Complete Psychological Works,* vol. 14. Edited by James Strachey et al. London: Hogarth Press, 1957.

Friedman, Maurice; Glasser, Mervin; Laufer, Eglé; Laufer, Moses; and Wohl, Myer. "Attempted Suicide and Self-Mutilation in Adolescence: Some Direct Observations from a Psychoanalytic Research Project." *International Journal of Psychoanalysis* 53:179–184 (1972).

Friedman, Paul, ed. *On Suicide: With Particular Reference to Suicide among Young Students.* New York: International Universities Press, 1967. (Discussions of the Vienna Psycho-Analytic Society, 1910.)

Friedman, Paul. "An Individual Act." In *On the Nature of Suicide,* edited by E. S. Shneidman. San Francisco: Jossey-Bass, 1969.

Garfinkel, B. D., and Golombek, H. "Suicide and Depression in Childhood and Adolescence." *Canadian Medical Association Journal* 110:1278–1281 (1974).

Glaser, Kurt. "The Treatment of Depressed and Suicidal Adolescents." *American Journal of Psychotherapy* 32(2):252–269 (1978).

Gould, Robert E. "Suicide Problems in Children and Adolescents." *American Journal of Psychotherapy* 19:228–246 (1965).

Gradolph, Philip C. "Developmental Vicissitudes of the Self and Ego Ideal During Adolescence." Presented at the Fall Meeting of the American Psychoanalytic Association, December 1978.

Haim, A. *Adolescent Suicide.* New York: International Universities Press, 1974.

Hankoff, L. D., and Einsidler, Bernice. *Suicide: Theory and Clinical Aspects.* Littleton: PSG Publishing, 1979.

Hendin, Herbert. "Student Suicide: Death as a Life Cycle." *Journal of Nervous and Mental Diseases* 10:204–219 (1975).

———. "Suicide: The Psychosocial Dimension." *Suicide and Life-Threatening Behavior* 8:99–117 (1978).

Hillman, James. *Suicide and the Soul.* New York: Harper and Row, 1964.

Hirsh, Joseph. "Suicide, Part 3: Dynamics of Suicide." *Mental Hygiene* 44:274–280 (1960).

Holinger, P. D. "Violent Deaths among the Young: Recent Trends in Suicide, Homicide, Accidents." *American Journal of Psychiatry* 136:1144–1147 (1979).

Honig, Sylvia. "Ideation in the Art Work of Suicidal Patients." *Art Psychotherapy* 2(1):77–85 (1975).

Jacobs, Jerry. *Adolescent Suicide.* New York: John Wiley and Sons, 1971.

Jacobson, Edith. *The Self and the Object World.* New York: International Universities Press, 1964.

———. "The Regulation of Self-Esteem." In *Depression and Human Existence,* edited by James E. Anthony and Therese Benedek. Boston: Little, Brown, 1975.

Kastenbaum, Robert, and Aisenberg, Ruth. *The Psychology of Death.* New York: Springer, 1972.

Kiell, Norman. *The Universal Experience of Adolescence.* New York: International Universities Press, 1964.

Klagsbrun, Francine. *Youth and Suicide: Too Young to Die.* New York: Pocket Books, 1977.

Kohut, H. *The Analysis of the Self.* New York: International Universities Press, 1971.

———. "Thoughts on Narcissism and Narcissistic Rage." *Psychoanalytic Study of the Child* 27:360–400 (1972).

Kreider, Douglas G., and Motto, Jerome A. "Parent-Child Role Reversal and Suicidal States in Adolescence." *Adolescence* 9:365–370 (1974).

Lampl-De Groot, J. "Ego Ideal and Superego." *Psychoanalytic Study of the Child* 17:94–106 (1962).

Leonard, Calista V. *Understanding and Preventing Suicide.* Springfield: Charles C. Thomas, 1967.

Lester, Gene, and Lester, David. *Suicide: The Gamble with Death.* Englewood Cliffs: Prentice-Hall, 1971.

Litman, Robert. "Sigmund Freud and Suicide." In *Essays in Self-Destruction,* edited by E. S. Shneidman. New York: Science House, 1967.

Lourie, Reginald S. "Clinical Studies of Attempted Suicide in Childhood." *Clinical Proceedings of the Children's Hospital* (Washington) 22:163–173 (1966).

McAnarney, Elizabeth R. "Adolescent and Young Adult Suicide in the United States: A Reflection of Societal Unrest?" *Adolescence* 14(56): 765–774 (1979).

Madison, Arnold. *Suicide and Young People.* New York: Seabury Press, 1978.

Malmquist, Carl P. "Depressions in Childhood and Adolescence." *New England Journal of Medicine* 284(16):887–893 (April 22, 1971), 284(17): 955–961 (April 29, 1971).

Marks, Philip A., and Haller, Deborah L. "Now I Lay Me Down for Keeps: A Study of Adolescent Suicide Attempts." *Journal of Clinical Psychology* 33(2):390–400 (1977).

Mattsson, Ake; Seese, Lynne R.; and Hawkins, James W. "Suicidal Behavior as a Child Psychiatric Emergency." *Archives of General Psychiatry* 20:100–109 (1969).

Meyersburg, Herman A.; Ablon, Steven L.; and Kotin, Joel. "A Reverberating Psychic Mechanism in the Depressive Process." *Psychiatry* 37:372–386 (1974).

Miller, John P. "Suicide and Adolescence." *Adolescence* 10:11-24 (1975).

Miller, Mary Susan. "Teen Suicide." *Ladies' Home Journal,* February 1977. Reprinted as "Cries for Help: Adolescent Suicide" in *Independent School,* December 1977.

Murray, Henry A. "Dead to the World: The Passions of Herman Melville." In *Essays in Self-Destruction,* edited by E. S. Shneidman. New York: Science House, 1967.

Murray, John. "Narcissism and the Ego Ideal." *Journal of the American Psychoanalytic Association* 12:477–511 (1964).

Nin, Anaïs. *The Diary of Anaïs Nin,* vol. 1. New York: Harcourt, Brace and World, 1966.

Percy, Walker. *The Last Gentleman.* New York: Avon, 1978.

Poznanski, Elva, and Zrull, Joel P. "Childhood Depression: Clinical Characteristics of Overtly Depressed Children." *Archives of General Psychiatry* 23:8–15 (1970).

Reich, Annie. "Pathologic Forms of Self-Esteem Regulation." *Psychoanalytic Study of the Child* 15:215–232 (1960).

Ritvo, Samuel. "Late Adolescence: Developmental and Clinical Considerations." *Psychoanalytic Study of the Child* 26:241–263 (1971).

Rogers, Carl. *Freedom to Learn.* Columbus, Ohio: Charles E. Merrill, 1969.

Rosenkrantz, Arthur L. "A Note on Adolescent Suicide: Incidence, Dynamics and Some Suggestions for Treatment." *Adolescence* 13(50):209–214 (1978).

Schrut, Albert. "Suicidal Adolescents and Children." *Journal of the American Medical Association* 188(13):1103–1107 (1964).

———. "Some Typical Patterns in the Behavior and Background of Adolescent Girls Who Attempt Suicide." *American Journal of Psychiatry* 125:69–74 (1968).

Schulsinger, F.; Kety, S. S.; Rosenthal, D.; and Wender, P. H. "A Family Study of Suicide." In *Origin, Prevention and Treatment of Affective Disorders,* edited by M. Schou and E. Strömgren. London and New York: Academic Press, 1979.

Shaw, Charles R., and Schelkun, Ruth F. "Suicidal Behavior in Children." *Psychiatry* 28:157–168 (1965).

Shneidman, E. S., ed. *On the Nature of Suicide.* San Francisco: Jossey-Bass, 1969.

——. *Suicidology: Contemporary Developments.* New York: Grune and Stratton, 1976.

Shneidman, E. S. *Essays in Self Destruction.* New York: Science House, 1967.

Spruiell, Vann. "Narcissistic Transformations in Adolescence." *International Journal of Psychoanalytic Psychotherapy* 4:518–536 (1975).

——. "Three Strands of Narcissism." *Psychoanalytic Quarterly* 44:577–595 (1975).

——. "Freud's Concepts of Idealization." *Journal of the American Psychoanalytic Association* 27:777–792 (1979).

Stengel, Erwin. *Suicide and Attempted Suicide.* New York: Penguin Books, 1964.

Sugar, Max, ed. *Female Adolescent Development.* New York: Brunner/Mazel, 1979.

Tayler, Steve. "The Confrontation with Death and the Renewal of Life." *Suicide and Life-Threatening Behavior* 8(2):89–98 (1978).

Teicher, Joseph D., and Jacobs, Jerry. "Adolescents Who Attempt Suicide: Preliminary Findings." *American Journal of Psychiatry* 122:1248–1257 (1966).

Thomas, A.; Chess, S.; and Birch, H. G. *Temperament and Behavior Disorders in Children.* New York: International Universities Press, 1968.

Toolan, James M. "Suicide and Suicidal Attempts in Children and Adolescents." *American Journal of Psychiatry* 118:719–724 (1962).

——. "Suicide in Children and Adolescents." *American Journal of Psychotherapy* 29(3):339–344 (1975).

——. "Therapy of Depressed and Suicidal Children." *American Journal of Psychotherapy* 32(2):243–251, 1978.

Van Del, Richard A. "The Role of Death Romanticization in the Dynamics of Suicide." *Suicide and Life-Threatening Behavior* 7(1):45–56 (1977).

Warren, Max. "On Suicide." *Journal of the American Psychoanalytic Association* 24(1):199–234 (1976).

Wechsler, James. *In a Darkness.* New York: W. W. Norton, 1972.

Wenz, Friedrich V. "Economic Status, Family Anomie, and Adolescent Suicide Potential." *Journal of Psychology* 98(1):45–47 (1978).

——. "Self Inquiry Behavior, Economic Status and the Family Anomie Syndrome among Adolescents." *Adolescence* 14(54):387–398 (1979).

Zilboorg, Gregory. "Considerations on Suicide with Particular Reference to That of the Young." *American Journal of Orthopsychiatry* 7:15–31 (1937).

We would like to acknowledge our many debts to friends and family:

For help in research and manuscript preparation, Jancis Long, Margaret Ledin, Pearl Levy, Elinor Weeks, and most especially, Patricia Carr and Constance May

For readers who sustained us with their enthusiasm, Steven Ablon, Judy Arnold, Rhonda Phalen, Joan and Laurie Cormay, Jenny Rose, colleagues at Cambridge Hospital Department of Psychiatry, the Cambridge-Somerville Mental Health and Retardation Center

For supporting us with his initial interest, former Little, Brown editor Llewellyn Howland

For keen editorial comment, Kate White, Freddy Hickler

For arranging our collaboration, Danny Mack

For teaching us about adolescence, our children — Danny, Kenny, Tony, Peter, Kate, Mark, Lisa, and Freddy

For their special part in making our manuscript a reality, Jean and Heidi Elshtain, Tyche Hendricks, Kate White, Jackie Lowe, Jenny Elshtain, Timothy May, Anne Tucker

For service and devotion through all the vicissitudes of our work, our editors, Roger Donald and Melissa Clemence

For the love and support of our spouses, Fred and Sally

And finally, our deepest gratitude to David, Paulette, Rob, and Laurel Loomis, to whom our book is dedicated